This *book belongs* to:

ROYAL TEAS

WITH

Grace and Style

ROYAL TEAS
with
GRACE AND STYLE

by

EILEEN SHAFER

DORRANCE PUBLISHING CO., INC.
PITTSBURGH, PENNSYLVANIA 15222

ISBN: 978-1-4349-0467-6

Printed in the United States of America

First Printing

For more information or to order additional books, please contact:
Dorrance Publishing Co., Inc.
701 Smithfield Street
Pittsburgh, Pennsylvania 15222
U.S.A.
1-800-788-7654
www.dorrancebookstore.com

Table *of* Contents

PREFACE 2

INTRODUCTION 4

1. TIDBITS OF TEA HISTORY 8

2. TEA VARIETIES 12

3. PREPARING TEA 16

4. LISTS AND DETAILS 22

5. INVITATIONS 28

6. PLANNING A TEA MENU 32

7. CREATING AN INVITING ATMOSPHERE 36

8. SETTING A BEAUTIFUL TEA TABLE 40

9. MANNERS MATTER 44

10. COURSE ONE: 52
    Recipes for Tea Sandwiches & Spreads

11. COURSE TWO: 62
    Recipes for Scones, Shortbread & Tea Breads

12. COURSE THREE: 78
    Recipes for Cookies, Cakes & other Sweets

13. TEA AND BEVERAGE RECIPES 110

ACKNOWLEDGEMENTS 119

DEDICATION

In loving memory of my grandmothers,
Adeline Evangelista-Catania
&
Cecelia Davidson-Walters,
both of whom exhibited grace and style.

"I am a hardened and shameless *tea drinker,*
who has, for twenty years, diluted his meals with only the infusion
of this fascinating plant; whose kettle has scarcely time to cool;
who with tea muses the evening, with tea *solaces* the midnight,
and with tea *welcomes* the morning."

-SAMUEL JOHNSON (1709 — 1784)

PREFACE

TRADITIONS are the establishment and passing down of rituals that nurture us while setting examples from one generation to another. A tradition may be something as simple as a menu we prepare for special occasions, a favorite place we return to, or an activity or event we enjoy repeating. Traditions also include special moments we look forward to sharing with family and friends.

FOR nearly two centuries, afternoon tea has become an established tradition, symbolic of British royalty and the quintessential formality of a by-gone era. The required social graces associated with this endearing ceremony encourage gentility and inspire us to create an impressive setting, while surrounding ourselves with those we love and things we treasure.

OVER many millennium of social development, tea ceremonies have survived the test of time. Their popularity transcends Asian cultures and remains an elegant affair, reminiscent of the Victorian era, where extraordinary care and service were reserved almost exclusively for people of high social status and great wealth. When the industrial revolution ushered in ways to make travel, tea, and tea wares more affordable to the common household, afternoon tea became an enlightening discovery across every continent.

TODAY, however, an ordinary afternoon can be transformed into a page from the past when presenting delicate china, sparkling crystal, and gleaming silver atop freshly starched linens, defining the ultimate art of entertaining in its finest hour. Preparing for such an occasion is truly a labor of love; from the gathering of special guests to the careful preparation of flavorful tea blends and delectable foods, taking tea is a dignified process, allowing precious time for peace, comfort and reflection. The proper etiquette and procedures in which afternoon tea is presented and served captures gracious living, and is indeed a charming celebration all its own.

INTRODUCTION

OVER the course of many years, I have been researching and sensationalizing images apparent to the customs and menus that are reflective of afternoon tea. It is a subject on which so much has already been written. The culmination of serving tea, entertaining with ease, and depicting a lovely scene for this event has become a passionate pursuit that I feel compelled to share with others.

FORMAL entertaining can be (at times) a bit intimidating, to say the least, but this book is designed to help you prepare for an afternoon tea, while putting fears to rest when serving a proper tea fit for a queen. There is nothing mysterious about entertaining graciously; it is simply adhering to some basic guidelines and having the desire to do so. The only secrets to entertaining well lie in planning ahead and making your guests feel comfortable. By planning your time carefully and putting forth every effort in creating a beautiful atmosphere, you can accomplish the three basic ingredients necessary when hosting your own successful afternoon tea: Time Effort Atmosphere

HINTS of making afternoon tea popular again were just beginning to resurface in America around the mid to late 1980s, while I was working as an interior designer and managing an exquisite retail store in a posh suburb of Chicago. What happened next helped lead me down a path I was destined to follow. In the spring of 1987, I was invited to accompany my employer on a business trip to New York, whose goal was to search for vintage millinery accessories to create exclusive designs for her store. It was there where we met a woman who introduced us to a periodical which premiered that very week: Good Housekeeping's Victoria Magazine. Then editor Nancy Lindemeyer beckoned readers to "Return to Loveliness," exhibiting the timeless elegance of living graciously and comfortably in English style, featuring reproduction fabrics, antique wares, tea accessories, and more. Because we had already been working with many English fabrics and had recently been introduced to a new trend in accessories, wired ribbons, we were ecstatic to find a magazine that mirrored the store's image and style. Savoring that very first issue of Victoria and those to follow, I immediately sensed that the revival of afternoon tea would once again be reinstated into American culture. My instincts were correct and I stayed the course.

SHORTLY after the birth of my daughter, Katie, I began a custom basket business out of my home and noticed that a resurgence of quality teas and tea-related items were successfully forging their way through gourmet food shows and retail gift markets. At that point, it was not enough for me to just apply a certain look and style to afternoon tea and my tea baskets. I then became committed, connecting the ancient brew to its legendary roots and established traditions before realizing one of my many dreams.

IN 1996 I set forth a business plan and a vision. With the help and support of a loving family and fantastic friends, I became the proprietor of a charming tea shop, nestled alongside the historic Fox River in my home town of St. Charles, Illinois. Serving English-style teas and offering daily tea tastings soon became second nature to me as I conquered selling a wide variety of loose leaf tea blends to patrons not yet familiar with proper brewing techniques or the pleasures of partaking in afternoon tea rituals. Within a few short months of my new venture, a very supportive community asked me to present a short narrative about 18th century tea history (at a school fair) for fifth grade students who were studying the Boston Tea Party and Revolutionary War. When parents of those students welcomed my presentation, I was asked to prepare another program, detailing hosting and serving of a proper afternoon tea at home. I was initially terrified at the thought of addressing an audience, but quickly resolved my fear of public speaking by becoming more knowledgeable and well-prepared on matters relating to tea's historic evolution. So in between running a retail business and serving afternoon teas in my shop, I became a voice of authority to expectant audiences, discussing time-honored traditions, demonstrating proper brewing methods, and presenting tablescapes in various historic settings. (Those initial speaking engagements gave me the confidence to prepare dozens more programs to hundreds of tea aficionados over the last 12 years.)

LIFE was good, but eventually demanding retail hours began restricting my new-found passion for tea talk, and I made a heart-wrenching decision to close my shop, concentrating my efforts on writing and lecturing about tea. There are days when I still miss my lovely tea shop and loyal patrons, but, consequently, the choice I made to pursue other venues has provided me with some very favorable results.

SINCE closing my shop, I have been afforded many opportunities to travel and take tea at quaint tea rooms, country inns, and luxury hotels across this great nation of ours. As a guest speaker, I have had the distinct honor of presenting informative tea talks to ladies' club groups, tea rooms, libraries, and history museums. The many pathways leading me to publishing my first book have been an incredible journey.

THE end result, in part, is a tribute to our historical social development, the ceremony of tea itself, as well as the traditions we value. This book is intended for anyone who loves teatime as I do, for those of you who may have an interest in hosting an afternoon tea, or for those who will have the extreme privilege and honor of attending one.

MAY some of my own personal experiences and favorite teatime recipes help guide and encourage you to relax and enjoy your own Royal Teas with Grace and Style.

Eileen Shafer

"There are few hours in my *life*
more *agreeable* than
the hour dedicated to
the *ceremony* known
as Afternoon Tea."

-HENRY JAMES

TIDBITS OF TEA HISTORY

"So great was his passion for tea that Mr. Jefferson designed a specific
polygonal-shaped Tea Room at his beloved Monticello ...
In his Tea Room, upon the small lap desk he had designed,
he wrote and edited the draft of the Declaration of Independence in 1776."

-BEULAH MUNSHOWER SOMMER AND PEARL DEXTER
TEA WITH PRESIDENTIAL FAMILIES

ALTHOUGH I make every effort to continue educating myself on the history of tea, I am nonetheless always in search of perfecting the next tea party. You need not be a historian to serve or enjoy a wonderful cuppa, but I do feel it is important to understand some basic tea history and pertinent information about the way in which tea is termed and served before hosting or attending an afternoon tea. Sharing interesting facts about the evolution of tea often stimulates some very interesting conversation among guests.

Tea in China

LEGEND has it that the Chinese Emperor, Shen Nung, made an unprecedented discovery in 2737 B.C., when leaves from a nearby Camellia sinensis bush dropped into his pot of boiling water. After drinking the flavorful brew, the concept of tea was born!

Tea in England

DURING the early part of the 19th century, Anna, the Seventh Duchess of Bedford, is credited with originating afternoon tea to ward off the hunger pangs between lunch and the customary late supper. Over time, friends joined her (in her private chambers) in the practice of taking tea and light refreshments which soon became steeped in tradition and tea party recipes.

IN the late 18th century the Earl of Sandwich had requested putting meats and cheeses between two slices of bread. This and other culinary creations led to the British custom of taking tea and little sandwiches in the afternoon.

QUEEN VICTORIA helped make the ritual of afternoon tea even more popular during the Victorian Era, so named after Her Royal Majesty, when rules of tea time etiquette and the use of proper tea wares were formally established. Throughout her extended six decade reign, the Queen was known for having an insatiable appetite and fondness for tea.

Tea in America

DURING the latter part of the 17th century, tea started gaining notoriety in America. At the dawn of the new century, imported items such as exotic fruits, spices, china, and fabrics found their way to the New World. Tea was often used as a commodity of trade along with those goods. In 18th century Colonial America, tea was considered a luxury item or a wealthy man's drink, and was locked in tea chests, carefully guarded by the head of the household to prevent servants from consuming or stealing it.

The Boston Tea Party

HISTORY relays that the high tax imposed on the colonists for imported tea helped trigger the Revolutionary War. On December 16th, 1773, Samuel Adams and his loyal group of patriots, known as The Sons of Liberty, disguised themselves as Native Indians and boarded the decks of three British ships docked in the Boston Harbor. They discarded 342 chests of tea into the water as an act of defiance and anger for the tax imposed upon them by the British Parliament. Although Boston was most famous for having caused this unprecedented rebellion, other harbors refusing tea included: Annapolis, Maryland; Charleston, South Carolina; Eddington, North Carolina; Greenwich, New Jersey; Philadelphia, Pennsylvania; and New York Harbor.

ICED TEA was recorded to have been served by residents in the South prior to 1890 but was introduced and popularized in 1904 at the St. Louis World's Fair by a tea merchant named Richard Blechynden. Due to scorching summer temperatures, this savvy but desperate American salesman had to devise a way to entice tourists to sample his teas. People ignored the hot beverages offered and began craving something cold and refreshing, therefore embracing the idea of tea over ice. According to current statistics, eighty percent of all tea consumed in the United States is served over ice.

THE TEABAG made its debut around 1908, when Thomas Sullivan, another innovative tea merchant, created silk pouches in order to send samples to his customers. As the bags grew in popularity, the modern teabag was developed in 1937 by Fay Osborne, who designed the paper version which is still manufactured by the Dexter Corporation to this day. In recent years, however, some gourmet tea companies are using silk-like sachets to present their fine line of loose-leaf teas for individual servings.

TIMES & TERMS USED TO DESCRIBE THE *Service* OF TEA

HIGH TEA is a term often used by Americans referring to an early evening tea event, seated at a formally set table with a menu consisting of a main entrée. The true British interpretation of high tea, however, surfaced in the 19th century as a working-man's early supper. The meal was usually quite substantial. It was called "high" tea because it was often taken sitting atop high stools in a tea shop or standing at a high counter. Whatever you choose to call it, high tea is never served before 5 o'clock.

AFTERNOON TEA has always been considered an elegant affair and is customarily served at 4 o'clock. In America, most hotels serve tea between 3 o'clock and 5 o'clock daily, while tearooms and country inns may offer tea and sandwiches as early as 1 o'clock on specified days. Along with a selection of fine teas, afternoon tea traditionally includes three food courses:

THE FIRST COURSE includes tea sandwiches or other savories.

THE SECOND COURSE includes tea breads, shortbread, and scones.

THE THIRD COURSE includes desserts.

THE FOURTH COURSE is added when sherry or champagne is served and is referred to as a ROYAL TEA.

A ROYAL TEA is also referred to by many tearooms when a non-alcoholic sparkling beverage is offered on their selective tea menus.

A LIGHT TEA requires only scones and desserts be served with tea.

A CREAM TEA requires only scones with jam and clotted cream be served with tea.

Because the practice of afternoon tea is cloaked in centuries of tradition, it is easy to understand the importance of serving or partaking in this ritual with grace and style.

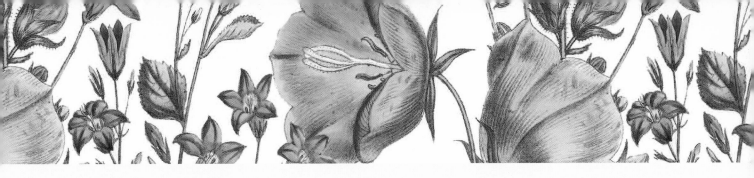

TEA VARITIES

"*There* is a great deal of poetry and
fine sentiment in a chest of *tea*."

RALPH WALDO EMERSON (1803 – 1882)
LETTERS AND SOCIAL AIM

I CALLED UPON one of the most distinguished tea experts and master tea blenders in America, Mr. John Harney, of Harney & Sons Fine Teas, for advice in relaying information that characterizes certain blends of some of the most popular teas served with afternoon tea menus. Mr. Harney implied that there are four recognized varieties of tea: black, green, oolong, and white. Teas differ according to preparation and oxidation of the leaves. Black tea leaves are fermented while green tea leaves are not. Oolong and Jasmine teas are created from a blend and is partially fermented. White tea is actually plucked (by hand) from the buds of the leaves which have not opened or revealed themselves to sunlight.

TEA can only be called tea when it is derived from the plant known as Camellia sinensis. As previously mentioned, tea is indigenous to China, but today many other countries, including India, Africa, Japan, and more recently the United States, produce many fine teas, with over 3000 types of teas available. However, tea should never be confused with the label "herbal tea" or tisanes. Herbal tea is created by blending herbs, flowers, or spices, but does not contain leaves from the actual Camellia sinensis plant. A tisane is an infusion of dried herbs which is sometimes used as a beverage for medicinal purposes and does not contain any tea leaves.

OVER the past two decades, tea has become one of the fastest growing industries in America and because of its worldwide popularity, consumers have many varieties to choose from and many ways in which to enjoy it. Scientific evidence supports a link between tea and a healthy lifestyle, but whatever your reason for drinking tea, enjoy it for all its benefits and many flavors.

SOME of the most requested, teas, herbal teas and tisanes include the following blends:

ENGLISH BREAKFAST is pure Chinese tea or India and/or Ceylon tea with a strong taste. Recommended steeping time is 5 minutes.

IRISH BREAKFAST is made from Assam tea and has a malty flavor. Recommended steeping time is 5 minutes.

DARJEELING is considered the "champagne of teas" and is grown in the Himalayan foothills. Due to its cost, Darjeeling is mostly used in blends, resulting in a lighter color and delicate taste. Recommended steeping time is 5 minutes.

ORANGE PEKOE OR CEYLON is a basic, large leaf black tea grown in India. Recommended steeping time is 4-5 minutes.

EARL GREY is a blend of large leaf teas from China and India, infused with bergamot oil, which produces a distinctive citrus flavor. Recommended steeping time is 5-6 minutes.

LAPSANG SOUCHONG is a large leafed tea with an intense smoky flavor. Recommended steeping time is 5-6 minutes.

OOLONG is lighter in flavor and color, the compromise between black and green leaves. Recommended steeping time is 5-6 minutes.

❋ All black teas and oolong teas require a full rolling boil to infuse tea leaves properly.

GUNPOWDER GREEN is hand-rolled from China and resembles a pellet shape. It is yellow in color with a light and refreshing taste. Recommended steeping time is 3 minutes.

SENCHA, a popular green tea from Japan, is grassy tasting, containing little caffeine and is said to have great health benefits. Recommended steeping time is 3 minutes.

❋ Green Teas require a boiling temperature of 180 degrees to 190 degrees Fahrenheit.

WHITE TEA usually comes from China. Recommended steeping time is 4-5 minutes.

CHAMOMILE is a floral tisane with a crisp scent, often referred to as sleepy-time tea. Recommended steeping time is 5 minutes.

LEMON VERBENA is a traditional French herbal tisane with a lemon flavor. Recommended steeping time is 5 minutes.

❋ White teas require a boiling temperature of 200 degrees Fahrenheit, whereas

❋ Chamomile and Lemon Verbena require a boiling temperature of 212 degrees Fahrenheit.

MANY tea companies produce other fine blends, which include fruited flavors such as peach, apricot, blackberry, black current, raspberry, apple, pear, cranberry, plum, and even pomegranate. They are usually black or green tea based, can contain bits and pieces of dried fruits or may be infused with natural fruit oils or artificial flavorings.

AT certain times of the year, holiday blends are a popular choice. These tea blends contain spices such as vanilla, almond, cinnamon, or cloves, with bits of dried orange and lemon rinds to compliment the various spices.

THERE are many flavors and blends available to satisfy just about everyone. I suggest selecting at least three varieties when serving afternoon tea, offering a different blend with each course. I often choose my teas to compliment the foods I am preparing, just as you would take the time to select fine wines to accompany a dinner menu. Many people struggle with health issues these days and may have dietary restrictions where caffeine is concerned; it is wise to offer guests an herbal tea or a decaffeinated blend as one of your selections.

TEA STORAGE and Buying Tips: Keep all teas airtight, free from strong odors, humidity and light. If possible, store tea in tins. Do not store tea in a refrigerator or freezer. A cool, dark place, away from heat, sunlight and spices will keep teas fresher. Black teas will last a long time when stored properly. Purchase teas more often and in small amounts. Green teas, however, are an exception. Freshness is important. Green teas should be used within 6 months.

SAMPLING TEAS: Many tea shops and gourmet supermarkets promote freshly brewed tea samples or may offer a sample or two to try at home. The best way to know if you are in agreement to certain blends is to smell the tea and trust your senses. If this is not possible, ask for recommendations or carefully check the ingredients listed on the package before making a purchase.

HELPFUL HINTS

Some companies produce teabags that contain bits and pieces from the tea leaves
and not the full tea leaves themselves. The tea in bags is sometimes
referred to as the dust from the tea leaves.

The term agony of the tea leaves is used to describe the unfolding
of the tea leaves when subjected to boiling water.

PREPARING TEA

"Sweet *tea* wasn't something that you whipped up in an instant.

If you took shortcuts, you'd end up with something cloudy and bitter.

Southern sweet tea was like Southern life – it was all the *richer*

and sweeter because we took time to do it right."

-DEBORAH FORD

PUTTIN' ON THE GRITS

IF you are not accustomed to brewing loose leaf teas, you may want to practice making a pot or two prior to hosting a tea party. It is very important to own a good tea kettle or an electric boiling pot which will allow the water to reach specific temperatures needed to infuse tea leaves properly. Use these kettles and pots for boiling water only. Never use a coffee pot to boil water for tea. Oils from the coffee beans will remain in the coffee pot no matter how clean you keep it and the residues will alter the taste of your tea.

UNLESS you are quite familiar with your own taste and that of your guests, it is my suggestion to check the directions on the package of tea you have purchased which should give instructions for boiling temperatures and steeping times. Teas require different boiling points to properly infuse the leaves. Most black teas require a full rolling boil before placing the tea leaves into the pot. Green teas, white teas, herbal teas, and tisanes require various temperatures as specified in the previous chapter. Although there are many recommendations for brewing hot tea, this is my personal advice for preparing the perfect pot of hot, loose-leaf tea:

PREPARING THE PERFECT POT OF HOT TEA

To begin, use fresh, purified drinking water.

Measure out how many cups you want to make and pour the
water into a clean tea kettle or an electric boiling pot.

Bring the water to a full boil or the correct temperature according to tea instructions.

Use 1 heaping measuring teaspoon per cup.
(Do not use an eating utensil teaspoon to measure tea, since they vary in sizes.)
If you prefer your tea a bit stronger, add one more heaping teaspoon for the pot.

Just as the water reaches the correct temperature, remove the kettle from the heat source.
(Do not over boil the water or it loses oxygen and your tea will taste flat.)

Place the loose tea inside the kettle to steep for the recommended time and set a timer.
(Do not judge the tea's strength by its color as some tea blends brew lighter than others.)

While your tea is steeping, fill your serving teapot with plain boiled water or very hot
tap water and let it sit in the serving pot while the loose tea steeps in the brewing pot.

Discard the hot water from your serving pot just before transferring the brewed tea.

Using a tea strainer over the serving pot, pour the brewed tea over the strainer to catch
any tea leaves from entering the serving pot. (This process is called decanting the tea.)

Put the lid back on the teapot and cover the teapot with a tea cozy until ready to serve.

Note: If wet tea leaves remain in the bottom of the teapot, there will be a significant
difference in taste when pouring the next or final cup of tea. The flavor becomes
stronger and sometimes bitter the longer it continues to steep.

AFTER many years of serving tea, I find that the overwhelming majority of Americans prefer to have their tea decanted. We know to remove our teabags from our cups when it has finished steeping, so why not separate the loose tea leaves from the liquid? Some tea leaves/blends may be used for a second or even a third steeping. In this case, reuse the wet leaves by adding more boiled water to the brewing pot and steep it again for the recommended time but decant it once more as you did the first time.

WHEN enjoying tea out in a special tearoom or luxury hotel, it is not uncommon, nor is it considered rude to request the server to decant your tea. Most hotels are instructed to offer more hot water to the teapot unless otherwise specified. Many tearooms across America are incorporating the use of teapots with removable baskets or plungers, another effective way of decanting the tea. The plunger teapots are referred to as tea presses, stopping the infusion of tea leaves when plunged.

IF you still remain uncomfortable with brewing loose tea, by all means use good quality teabags or sachets. Many gourmet tea companies are producing wonderful teabags/sachets, in which full tea leaves are used. But if you elect to offer your guests teabags/sachets during your tea party, be prepared to have an attractive waste bowl available for disposing used bags and wrappers. Discretely empty and clean the waste bowl while your guests are chatting away before offering them a second teabag/sachet. Do not squeeze the teabag/sachet or leave used teabags/sachets next to your cup, on saucers. Use the common waste bowl. In the event of a seated tea, the hostess may make individual teabag holders available at each guest's place setting.

Preparing Iced Tea

If the temperature outside is more suiting for tea over ice, follow these simple
tips for making the perfect gallon of iced tea, using loose-leaf tea:

Use one gallon of purified drinking water, preferably room temperature.

Pour 5-6 cups of water into a clean tea kettle or an electric boiling pot
and bring the water to the recommended temperature.

Remove from the heat source and place up to 1 ounce of loose tea leaves in the brewing pot.
(The amount of tea used will depend upon how strong you like your tea; keep in mind
if the tea becomes too strong, you may always add more water or ice to dilute it.)

Let the tea leaves steep for 10 minutes. Set a timer.

Using a tea strainer, pour the brewed tea over the strainer and into a pitcher
or other container, with the remaining water, to equal one gallon.

Refrigerate tea or immediately add ice to freshly brewed tea.

Preparing Sweet Tea

IN the southern states, sweet tea is THE beverage of choice. When making sweet tea at
home, place desired amount of sugar in the pitcher with the warm freshly brewed tea so the
granulated sugar can dissolve easily. If you do not wish to sweeten the tea ahead of time, offer your
guests liquid sugar (on the side) eliminating the grainy granulated sugar from settling at the
bottom of the glass once the tea is cold. (Recipe for liquid sugar can be found in Tea and Beverage
Recipes.) Do not use sugar cubes in iced tea as they do not dissolve well in cold
beverages; they are meant to be used in hot tea.

HELPFUL HINTS

It is best to use room temperature water before brewing iced tea. This along
with purified drinking water usually insures crystal clear tea. If your iced tea
becomes cloudy after refrigeration, add a tablespoon or two of very hot
or boiled water to the tea. This should help it become clear again.

LISTS AND DETAILS

"There is no *trouble* so great or grave that cannot
be much diminished by a *nice* cup of tea."

-BERNARD-PAUL HEROUX,
1900S BASQUE PHILOSOPHER

YOU would not attend an important business meeting without giving it considerable thought and preparation. Nor would you ever conceive of trying out for a sporting event without some coaching or perform at a music recital without practicing beforehand. If you intend to host an afternoon tea you need to understand the importance of teatime etiquette and the preparation involved, both of which are essential to insure your party's success and, most of all, making your guests feel special.

IF you are like me, you cannot function without a detailed list of what is needed for a party. It helps to be well organized. When I have a written or printed list in front of me, I can easily prioritize and check things off when completed. I have recently taken to storing files in my computer in the event I should lose or misplace anything important. This also saves time should I need to refer to anything for future parties. Here are some suggestions that have helped me when preparing for afternoon teas:

1. *Guest List* – ADDRESSES, PHONE NUMBERS, RSVPS

Make a list of friends and family you would like to invite to tea but create an interesting mix of people who would enjoy spending a special afternoon together. Make sure you have enough room in your home to comfortably seat each guest you intend to invite whether you plan to serve buffet-style or at a seated table. Locate addresses and phone numbers prior to selecting invitations. This will save time once invitations are ordered.

2. *Invitations* – STATIONERY STORE AND PHONE NUMBERS

Allow ample time for printing when selecting invitations. Always give your stationery store a deadline when invitations need to be returned, allowing yourself plenty of time to mail or deliver them. You may also ask that the merchant let you to take the envelopes home so you can address them while waiting for printing to be completed. Remember to pick up postage stamps or other embellishments required to complete your invitations.

3. *Menu* – TEAS AND COURSES
List foods and teas you plan to serve and pull all recipes needed.

4. *Ingredients Needed* – GROCERY LIST, STORES
After you have decided what sweets and savories you would like to make, list all ingredients and stores which will help you locate items needed for each recipe.

5. *Bakery/Caterer* – PHONE NUMBERS
If you intend to have special desserts made or prefer to have your party catered, contact your bakery or caterer as soon as possible with the date and time of your party and place orders early.

6. *Music/Muscians* – PHONE NUMBERS
When using CDs or stereo equipment, select your favorite music and make certain everything is in working order. If you elect to hire musicians such as a pianist, flutist, violist, or harpist, make contacts early to reserve your date. Most professional musicians require a deposit in advance, but high school or college students may offer to play, requesting that compensation be made the day of the performance. (Never underestimate the talent of students. I have hired music students to perform for many tea parties and special occasions. This also allows them added opportunities to perform in public.)

7. *Florist* – PHONE NUMBER
If you require special floral arrangements, contact your florist with colors and heights of arrangements as soon as you know how your table and rooms are to be set up.

8. *Helpers* – PHONE NUMBERS
If you require assistance the day of your party and have enlisted friends or family to help hang coats, prepare food trays, etc., keep names and phone numbers handy in the event you need to reach them with important information or details. Their duties should be discussed well in advance so they know when to arrive and what needs to be done.

9. Tea Wares and Accessories — OWNED, BORROWED OR RENTED
Such items may include, but are not limited to:

Tea kettle or boiling pot to brew tea

Teapot, creamer, and sugar bowl

Tea cozy

Teacups and saucers

Luncheon-size or dessert dishes

Three-tiered tray or serving platters

Water, wine, champagne glasses or stemware

Table linens, napkins, and doilies for platters

Teaspoons, spreaders, pastry/dessert forks, and iced teaspoons *(if necessary)*

Sugar tongs or sugar spoon *(sugar cubes or loose sugars)*

Lemon dish with fork for lemon slices

Small bowls for serving clotted cream and jams

Waste bowl *(if using teabags/sachets)*

Water pitcher

Punch bowl, ladle, punch cups

Candles

Fresh flowers

IF you do not possess all of these items, try borrowing dishes or serving pieces from friends or family members. Always remember to return things in the same, if not better condition than you received them. Otherwise, most rental stores provide many of these items as well as tables and chairs, should you need extras. Remember to stock cleaning supplies needed to clean your house and polish your silver and other serving pieces. Purchase these things early to eliminate last minute trips to the store.

To Do List:

This list is very important. Many projects can be done well in advance of your party. Below is a helpful guide to follow:

One Week Before:

Do as much shopping as possible for any and all items that will keep, such as teas, dry ingredients, candles, liquor, etc.

Three Days Before:

❋ Take out serving pieces that are to be used.
❋ Clean and polish silver and other serving pieces.
❋ Make or bake foods that can be stored or frozen in advance.
❋ Calls to guests who may not have responded to your invitation.

The Day Before:

❋ Pick up fresh ingredients such as milk, whipping cream, sour cream, fruits and herbs.
❋ Bake desserts that will keep fresh until the party.
❋ Prepare spreads and fillings for sandwiches.
❋ Wash all dishes, glassware, and silverware, or anything that has been stored in cabinets for long periods of time. Everything should be free of dust and sparkling clean when you are ready to set your tables.
❋ Clean your House. Arrange tables and serving pieces so you have an idea where everything will be placed. Contact your bakery, caterer, rental supplier, florist, or any helpers to make certain they are aware of the time you will need items ready to be picked up or delivered. Do not wait until the day of your party, in the event of a miscommunication. You do not want to deal with any errors or mishaps at the last minute.
❋ Plan what you are going to wear to your party (including jewelry) and set things out. Iron your outfit and clean your jewelry, if needed.

Last Minute:

❈ Keep scones wrapped, allowing them to come to room temperature before heating

oven.

❈ Measure water for tea kettles or boiling pots.

❈ Place milk (for tea) in pitcher and set out sugar bowl.

❈ Embellish food trays with greenery and flowers.

❈ Preheat oven for baking scones.

❈ Set out jam, lemon curd, and cream for scones.

❈ Light candles.

❈ Start the music prior to guests arriving.

❈ Put punch together or set out other beverages just prior to guests arriving.

❈ Brush egg wash or milk on scones and sprinkle with sugar before baking.

❈ Prepare tea while scones are baking.

WHEN I follow these examples and have a checklist in front of me, I feel more confident and prepared. Afternoon tea requires many items and a variety of foods that are not used or served on a daily basis. This is why I stress using a detailed list for this occasion so you are ready to greet your guests in a calm and collected manner.

INVITATIONS

"Thank God for Tea!
What would the *world* do without tea? How did it exist?
I am glad that I was not born *before* tea."

-REVERED SYDNEY SMITH
LADY HOLLAND'S MEMOIR

I HAVE a weakness for beautiful stationeries and confess to spending hours selecting and creating special invitations. There have been times when I planned a party just because I found gorgeous invitations I could not resist purchasing.

WHEN Anna Griffin committed to providing her outstanding artwork for my tea book, I was elated as I have been a fan of hers for many years. Although Anna is well known for introducing inprintable wedding invitations with a custom look, I have used some of her signature vellum and ribbon wedding invitations for afternoon tea invitations. Anna has created numerous other stationeries, cards, and scrapbooking papers that are also suitable for use as tea invitations. Many of Anna Griffin designs are available at select arts and crafts stores as well as fine stationery stores worldwide.

AS we enjoy a more casual society, it is becoming more customary to place a phone call or send an electronic message to guests, eliminating the hand-written or printed invitation. This is permissible if the tea is casual or impromptu, but when hosting a proper afternoon tea, neither of the first two procedures is an option. Invitations should be sent out or received at least two weeks in advance of your tea. A beautiful invitation sets the tone for any party, and will encourage guests to reply enthusiastically. There are almost as many selections of invitations available as there are tea blends; everything from fill-in-the blanks to lovely printed or engraved invitations, from whimsical to formal. I select invitations carefully as they relate to the season, theme, or formality of the party.

HAND-ADDRESSED envelopes are required for most any invitation. Although it may be practical to do so, banish any thought of using computerized labels for this occasion! Take time to address the envelope in your best penmanship. If your handwriting leaves something to be desired, try printing. If all else fails, call upon a friend or family member who has a great handwriting to do this for you, or, depending upon the importance and formality of your event, professional calligraphers may be hired to address envelopes. Many stationery stores offer guides (with lines) to place inside the envelope to ensure your writing stays on a straight line. These guides are often included with wedding invitations. If the envelope is lined, making it difficult to see through the paper, you must rely on a steady hand to address your envelopes. Any way you choose to do it, just remember that a beautifully addressed envelope is always appreciated and admired.

Here are a few suggestions for creating your own printed afternoon tea invitations:

If you are honoring someone at your tea, indicate so by using that person's name on the invitation:

Shirley Nichol

To honor

Patricia Kendrick

Afternoon Tea

Wednesday, October the twenty-sixth

Four o'clock

The Williamsburg Inn

Rockefeller Room

Williamsburg, Virginia

Please respond (757) 555-1515

If you are honoring a special celebration, you may use the following example:

Afternoon Tea

A Birthday Celebration

Honoring Phyllis

Monday, January 14th

Three o'clock

74 Braewood Drive

Algonquin, Illinois

R.S.V.P. Nancy Reinke (847) 555-1515

Another sample for a simply stated afternoon tea invitation might read:

Please join us for High Tea

Friday, November 7th

Five o'clock

1707 Windsor Court

Williamsburg, Virginia

Eileen and Katie

Regrets: (757) 555-1515   Formal attire requested

Use your imagination and be creative, but most of all, present your afternoon tea invitation with style.

PLANNING A TEA MENU

"Another *novelty* is the tea party, an extraordinary meal in that,
being offered to persons that have already dined well, it supposes neither appetite nor thirst,
and has no objection but distraction, no basis but *delicate* enjoyment."

-JEAN-ANTHELME BRILLAT-SAVARIN
THE PHYSIOLOGY OF TASTE

I HAVE BEEN SERVING afternoon teas for twenty years. I never tire of the menu choices, traditions, or friends and family with whom I share this hour. Planning an afternoon tea, however, is not as easy as it looks. It takes a lot of effort to make gracious entertaining appear effortless. This is why I encourage you to plan a menu that suits your own tastes and style so you will be able to greet your guests with confidence the day of your party.

I ENJOY preparing special menus and favorite foods, using tried and true recipes, but there have been occasions when time was not on my side and I had to call upon bakeries, delis, caterers, or ready-prepared foods to help me out. Disregard any notion that everything must be homemade in order to achieve success. If you haven't the flair for cooking or baking, but decorating your house and hosting a party are your true talents, then turn the food preparation over to the experts. Become familiar with your local food establishments. Make certain you call upon reliable merchants who provide the freshest ingredients possible. You may find delicious pastries from one bakery, but prefer cookies from another. Beautifully decorated cakes such as chocolate, carrot cake, coconut cake, cheesecakes, or butter pound cakes are quite popular for serving with tea, and are readily available at most specialty supermarkets or bakeries. Do not hesitate to use ready-prepared items (of good quality), which can be found in either the refrigerated or freezer sections of your favorite supermarkets. Either way, I have included some ideas and advice to help you prepare a special menu for afternoon tea.

AS MENTIONED EARLIER, afternoon tea is traditionally served in three courses, while offering one or more teas or a different blend of tea with each course. How many selections of tea you choose to serve is a personal choice.

COURSE ONE: Tea Sandwiches *(also referred to as Savories)*
Tea sandwiches should be petite, with crusts removed. They may be closed with fillings in between two slices of bread, or open-faced with cucumber, tomato, or salmon on top of one slice of miniature-shaped bread, toasted rounds, or crackers. Mini croissants or petite dinner rolls filled with chicken or tuna salad also make perfect tea sandwiches. The variety of fillings and shapes for tea sandwiches are only limited by your imagination.

COURSE TWO: Scones, Shortbread, and Tea Breads
Slightly sweetened scones are traditionally served, warm from the oven, slathered with strawberry jam and topped with clotted cream. Fruit breads and shortbread may be served in this course. Lemon curd and other flavored jams may also be used with scones and tea breads.

COURSE THREE: Desserts (also referred to as Tea Cakes)
This course includes cookies, pastries, tarts, cakes, or any other sweet dessert.

You may select as many different savories, breads, and sweets as you wish. Although foods for afternoon tea appear small and light, do not be deceived; these mini bites can be very filling. Here are suggestions for adequate servings per guest:

SANDWICHES: four to six little sandwiches per person

SHORTBREAD & TEA BREADS: one slice of each per person

SCONES: two per person if small; one per person if large

DESSERTS: one of each dessert per person

AGAIN, these are merely suggestions for adequate servings. I always plan to have more food available in the event guests simply want more. But keep in mind, afternoon tea is not considered a meal.

THE cream used for scones may be referred to as whipped cream, clotted cream, Devon cream, or Devonshire cream. Imported Devon and Devonshire creams (from England) are usually available in the refrigerated dairy section of most specialty and gourmet supermarkets. If you plan to use whipped cream, the cream should be freshly whipped the day of your party to ensure volume and freshness.

READY-PREPARED FAVORITES

I TRY to keep a few ready-prepared, name brand foods in my freezer as backup when I run out of time to prepare homemade goodies. I am happy to share the makers of some of my favorite products with you so you can always be ready for any last minute tea parties or emergencies. These items can be found in the frozen food sections or in the aisles of most grocery stores:

NANCY'S SPIRAL SANDWICHES
come frozen in various flavors such as tomato provolone, club sandwich, and turkey bacon ranch. These sandwiches only require defrosting.

NANCY'S PETITE QUICHES
come frozen in two of my favorite flavors; Lorraine (Swiss cheese with bacon and Florentine) and Swiss Cheese with Spinach. These quiches require a few minutes in the oven before serving and may then be served at room temperature.

ATHENS MINI FILLO SHELLS
come frozen but are fully baked for savories or sweets, ready to fill and serve.

DELIZZA PATISSERIE
Frozen Belgian Mini Cream Puffs only require a sprinkling of powdered sugar or chocolate sauce on top when thawed.

MRS. SMITH'S CARROT CAKE
is available in a small loaf and only requires defrosting and slicing.

SARA LEE'S FRENCH CREAM CHEESECAKE
comes frozen and requires thawing. This cheesecake may be sliced into bite-sized pieces or cut into shapes while partially frozen.

PEPPERIDGE FARM COOKIES
come packaged in a variety of flavors and shapes.

PEPPERIDGE FARM
Crème Filled Pirouette Rolled Wafers come in a cylinder-shaped tin in various flavors. These rolled cookies look especially pretty when served from a stemmed glass or an antique Spooner.

ONCE trays are decorated and embellished with fresh berries, flowers, or greenery, it will appear as though you put forth extraordinary efforts in presenting a beautiful afternoon tea. Again, you do not have to be a gourmet chef to host an afternoon tea with grace and style.

CREATING AN INVITING ATMOSPHERE

"A confused mind cannot direct deft hands, and what is more confusing than
a cluttered, disorderly place to work? What is more uninviting, too?
The *grateful* appearance of order – this is the one important way
women judge each other's housekeeping. And every efficient housekeeper
knows that in no room does it count for more than in the kitchen."

WOMAN'S HOME COMPANION, AUGUST 1924

A GRACIOUS HOME reflects personality and warmth in small ways: the smell of something baking in the oven, a pretty candlelit table set for company while music plays softly in the background. As often as I entertain and open my home to guests, there are times I admit to putting the finishing touches on things as guests are approaching my doorstep, but the bulk of my tasks are sufficiently completed well in advance of the party. Your house should be clean, foods should be prepared and ready to be set upon the table at least an hour before your party begins which should leave plenty of time to comfortably dress and still have a few minutes to critique everything on your lists before guests arrive. I have helped serve and cater many parties where the hostess was frantically cleaning or searching for needed items as I arrived with food. Here are some helpful tips to follow, alleviating last minute chaos.

FIRST and foremost it is important to receive guests in a well-groomed house. (Do not overlook cleaning and decorating your front porch or entry way.) Make arrangements in advance to clean your house the day before your party. Do not wait until the last minute to polish furniture or serving pieces. You may have to pick up a little or lightly go over things that day, but do not wear yourself out by leaving major cleaning until the last minute. Your kitchen should be spotless! This includes your refrigerator and ovens. Leave plenty of space on countertops for platters and serving pieces. Later on you will need a place to set aside used serving pieces, dishes, and teacups.

PREPARE a spot in your home for coats, purses, and umbrellas, if necessary. If coats are to be hung in a closet, that closet then needs to be tidy with enough hangers for each guest's coat. If you simply do not have room to hang extra coats, you may need to use one of your bedrooms for this purpose, but may wish to lay a blanket or a clean sheet on top of a bedspread before placing coats down. Rental facilities also supply coat racks and hangers. Have these things ready before your guests arrive.

TABLES may be arranged and set as early as the night before your party. If you are hosting a tea where designated seating is not necessary, leave enough space on side tables, coffee tables, and tea tables for guests to set down teacups, plates, and glasses. Be certain large floral arrangements, vases, or statues do not obstruct anyone's view when engaging in conversation.

YOUR main bathroom must be clean and inviting as this may be the first room that is needed, especially by guests who may have traveled a distance to attend your party. Provide guests with pretty hand towels, fragrant soaps, an extra roll of tissue paper, and room spray. If your master bathroom is off limits to guests, indicate so by leaving the door closed and/or locked.

LIGHT candles prior to guests arriving. There is nothing more inviting than a candlelit room, especially at dusk or on a gloomy day. Just remember to keep all candles safe from drafty areas and fans, and make certain flames are enclosed in proper candle holders. Never leave exposed candles unattended in rooms you do not plan to be in.

MUSIC for this occasion is a must. Any soft, contemporary, or classical music helps set the mood for any tea party. Whether you choose to use CDs or entertain guests with special musicians, there is nothing that exudes elegance more than lovely background music playing during afternoon tea.

IT helps to be well organized prior to the designated time, so you are at the door as your guests begin arriving. Greet them warmly. You only have one chance to make a first impression!

SETTING A BEAUTIFUL TABLE

"I can *imagine* myself sitting down at the head of the table and pouring out the tea,"
said Anne, shutting her eyes *ecstatically*, "And asking Diana if she takes sugar!
I know she doesn't, but of course I'll ask her just as if I didn't know."

-LUCY MAUD MONTGOMERY
ANNE OF GREEN GABLES

OLD things seem to have a personality all their own. If you collect antique silver, china, or glassware, teatime is the perfect occasion to share your unique treasures with those you choose to entertain. A tea table should be arranged with care and adorned with objects close to your heart. Some pieces speak for themselves and need only to be admired. I believe that a table should be set in the same fashion we dress ourselves: in layers, using runners, table scarves, and square toppers over the main tablecloth and selecting platters, and using decorative china and silver as we would accessorize ourselves with exquisite jewelry. If your invitation sets the tone for the party, then your beautiful tea table should set the stage and be an outstanding focal point in your room.

OVER the years I have had the pleasure of collecting many sets of dishes, from glassware to fine china, which enables me to change the look of my table more often. I also possess a collection of small antique pedestal cake stands and enjoy using these tinier versions for displaying items other than little cakes. I find there is nothing more elegant than showcasing silver on a tea table. Let your creativity shine when setting the tea table with your own special treasures.

IN LISTS AND DETAILS, I specify certain utensils which are traditionally needed to serve afternoon tea. Some of the items mentioned are necessities, while others are suggestions of pieces that may be used. It is really up to you to set the table, exhibiting your own taste and style. A mixture of patterns and unique serving pieces can provide a very interesting table setting. Everything does not have to match perfectly but remember to use dishes and serving platters that compliment one another. If you have inherited heirloom china, share it along with a story of how you came to own it. If you have a teacup collection, it is fun to use a variety of patterns and colors which will help guests easily identify their own cup throughout the party.

I ESPECIALLY LIKE using child-size silverware when serving tea. The smaller forks and spoons are perfect for petite tea foods and the small knife could easily serve as a spreader. Otherwise, offer salad forks, pastry forks and demitasse spoons to enhance the delicacy of the foods being served.

TABLE linens should be clean and crisp. White tablecloths are very traditional and include brocade, linen, and lace. Depending upon the dishes you choose to use and display or the season being celebrated, colorful table linens also work nicely. Small cloth tea napkins are required when serving afternoon tea. I have found a variety of tea napkins in antique stores and fine linen departments but I have also used pretty handkerchiefs since they are about the right size. If you do not own tea or luncheon-size napkins, avoid using dinner-size napkins. Instead use scalloped rice paper napkins; they not only come in a variety of solid colors and beautiful patterns, but are soft and durable as well. These or small cloth napkins may be fanned and placed through the finger holder of the teacup so each guest receives a napkin when tea is served. This is especially helpful when serving tea buffet-style as guests will already have their hands full with plates, teacups, and silverware. When seated at a set table, this ingenious device also eliminates the need to use napkins rings.

WHEN placing flowers on a tea table, almost any arrangement will do as long as the fragrance of flowers does not overpower the foods on the table. If you are to be formally seated at a table, do not order a tall arrangement which may obstruct anyone's view.

TAPERED or column candles set atop elegant candleholders showcase well on any formal table. However, when using scented candles, select fragrances that will not affect the flavors of foods on the table. It might be wise to light unscented candles on your food tables and use scented candles elsewhere throughout your house.

I ALWAYS SET a separate table for punch bowls and other beverages which are to be served as guests arrive. Using a fresh floral wreath to encircle a punch bowl adds texture and color to an otherwise plain table.

WHEN serving afternoon tea buffet-style, the teapot may also be served from a separate table to establish a flow as guests help themselves to foods. Your teapot, creamer, sugar bowl, lemon slices, and mint sprigs should always be within comfortable reach for you to serve guests or for guests to help themselves.

OTHER important items that should not be overlooked are embellishments to food trays. Edible flowers, greenery, fruits, and berries help to enhance bread and sandwich trays which tend to look somewhat plain by themselves. A ripe, uncut pineapple is naturally fragrant and could be used as a centerpiece or focal point for any table; atop a pedestal cake dish, surrounded by ivy, greenery, flowers, or fresh berries, a fresh pineapple can make a beautiful, yet simple statement.

ANOTHER lovely idea to compliment your table is to provide special place cards at each guests' setting. In the event you prefer serving buffet-style, place cards or a menu card may be used in front, behind, or to the side of platters, indicating what foods are being offered.

THERE are endless ways in which to set a beautiful tea table, displaying your own personal style.

MANNERS MATTER

"Etiquette is a code of behavior based on
consideration and *kindness*; and manners are the
outward evidence that we live by that code."

-MARTHA BISHOP
SOUTHERN LADY

ON a daily basis, we are more familiar and comfortable with casual gatherings, so for most of us elegant entertaining is quite a different experience where proper etiquette and exceptional manners are put to the ultimate test. Good manners are essential when dining out or when accepting an invitation to be entertained in someone's home, whether it is in a casual or formal setting. Always remember that proper manners never go out of style or lose charm.

The Perfect Hostess

WHEN hosting an afternoon tea I urge you to present your guests with the best of everything you have to offer while introducing your own unique style. Use the antique dishes, polish the silver, and get out the etched crystal stemware you have been displaying in your cabinet for years. Afternoon tea is truly a special occasion, worthy of your finest possessions. But keep in mind, with all the special efforts and formality that suits this occasion, your guests should always be made to feel relaxed and comfortable in your presence and in your home. Whether you choose to serve an intimate tea for two or entertain 50 guests, a good hostess is always gracious and well-prepared.

A HOSTESS must also understand that some guests may never have attended an afternoon tea and will be watching your every move to follow your lead. Your beautiful invitation will be your first opportunity to make a statement, setting the tone for the formality in which you will present yourself and your beautiful home.

Asking for Help

EVERY one of us has our own way of doing things, but it is not unheard of for a hostess to ask for help when needed. If you find yourself running short on time as guests begin arriving, ask a friend or relative to complete last minute tasks for you so you look prepared when greeting your guests. If a guest should arrive earlier than expected and offers to help you so you can attend to other things, feel free to give that person something to do; most friends and relatives feel the need to be needed.

Introductions

MAKE certain proper introductions are made but do not engage in lengthy conversation until everyone has arrived or until your guests are properly seated. If you have a guest demanding your undivided attention, graciously let him or her know that you have some last minute things to attend to, promising to be attentive once everything is completed.

IF you are honoring someone special at your tea, make certain your guest of honor is beside you as your guests arrive and personally introduce that person to each guest individually. Once all of your guests are seated or settled, present your honorary guest a second time, proceeding to explain the reason for recognizing that person. It is considered proper for a hostess to stand when introducing a guest of honor, acknowledging any titles or achievements befitting that person. A guest of honor may be someone as endearing as a new neighbor, a life-long friend, a family member, or perhaps a public figure.

Conversation

IT is the duty of any hostess to keep an engaging conversation alive. Avoid talking about unpleasant things, as negative conversation will distract from the lovely atmosphere you have created.

Tidiness versus Cleaning

IT is also your obligation (as hostess) to ensure that everyone has had enough to eat and drink, but never rush anyone. Afternoon tea is meant to be relaxing. When everyone has finished eating, you may clear tables of dirty plates, used teacups, and leftover food, but it is completely inappropriate to retreat to the kitchen to wash dishes. This should never be done while guests are still visiting. This is why you plan in advance to have designated helpers or simply leave the mess until everyone has departed.

Pouring Tea

AFTER the tea is properly steeped and on the table, it is appropriate for the hostess to pour the first cups. This provides a second chance to greet and welcome all of your guests. However, it is considered an honor to appoint a person to help pour the tea; this may be a close friend or family member but never ask the guest of honor to pour the tea. You may assist guests with sugar, milk, and lemon slices when tea is served buffet-style. If you are pouring tea at a seated and formally set table, you may assist guests with condiments or simply allow them to help themselves to sugar, milk, and lemon slices after you have poured the tea.

MOST tea spouts have a tendency to drip so be prepared and have a tea towel ready. In the event of a major spill or a broken teacup, blot the tea with your towel and apologize for the blunder. If you should splash or spill tea on a guest, sincerely apologize and direct your undivided attention to that guest immediately, but do not panic. Once your guest is attended to and settled, try to divert attention away from the unfortunate incident but continue to (discreetly) check on your guest throughout the party. The reason I share this with you is that this happened to me while serving tea to a customer in my shop. The tea poured out too fast and some of the hot tea spilled on her hand, causing some redness but not a severe burn. Accidents do happen, and it is important to be a hostess who is attentive and prepared for anything!

Hostess Gifts

A HOSTESS is not obligated to open any gifts during the party in the event not everyone brought something, therefore, making some guests feel uncomfortable. If a guest brings you a gift of tea, you need not serve it, as you may have chosen specific teas to suit your menu. Enjoy your gift of tea at a later time or invite that friend to share it with you at another time. Some gifts, such as fresh flowers, may require your immediate attention. If a fresh floral arrangement is presented to you, graciously accept them, but you need not display them on your tea table since you most likely have chosen your own arrangements and colors. Should you be given flowers that require cutting and/or arranging, thank your guest to show your appreciation and place them in water until you have time to arrange them later. Try to have a vase accessible so you do not have to hunt for one as guests are arriving. Or ask one of your friends to take care of this for you. This is why you plan in advance to have designated helpers.

EVEN though a hostess is giving the gift of hospitality to guests, it is an added touch to send guests home with a little remembrance of your special afternoon together. Your gift need only be a small token of thoughtfulness and need not be anything extravagant or expensive, just a little something to place at each person's setting or perhaps something left in a basket near the front door for guests to take as they leave your home. Your gift may include: a special truffle tucked inside a pretty little box, a dainty demitasse spoon tied with a ribbon, a tiny package of tea, or a printed menu card of what you served that afternoon, with a special recipe included. Any one of these gestures will leave a lasting impression of you as the perfect hostess.

Departures and Thank Yous

A GOOD HOSTESS should always see guests to the door when they leave the party and thank them for coming. Send a thank you note to each guest who brought any type of gift. This should be done within 2-3 days of the party.

The Perfect Guest

OVER the years, I have been a guest as many times as I have been a hostess. There is nothing more special than receiving an invitation to be entertained in someone's home for any occasion. In fact, it is a privilege. So here is some advice and suggestions on good guest etiquette.

Responding to an Invitation

WHEN an invitation to afternoon tea arrives, you should respond as soon as possible. Even if the invitation specifies "regrets only," it is considered proper to call and thank your hostess for inviting you. Do not wait until the day before the party or worse yet, the day of the party to respond to an invitation. If you think you may have a conflicting schedule, advise the hostess of your dilemma, provided that last minute arrangements are suitable to her. If arrangements in your schedule do change and you find you are able to attend, contact your hostess immediately. Do not leave your hostess waiting on your response.

Bringing a Hostess Gift

IT is a nice gesture to bring a hostess gift to show your appreciation for the invitation. If you know your hostess well, it should not be a problem choosing something he or she would like. If your hostess is an acquaintance, a small token such as a candle, a pretty tin of tea, a special box of chocolates, or a small seasonal item is acceptable. It need not be an elaborate gift. In presenting flowers, a pre-arranged vase or perhaps a small flowering house plant such as violets would be nice.

Introductions and Little Ladies

WHEN you arrive for tea, wait for your hostess to direct you where you are to go or where you are to be seated. If introductions to other guests are not formally made, feel free to introduce yourself. If the invitation includes children, do remember it is your responsibility to look after your little ones. Children (as well as adults) should not roam freely throughout someone's home or handle things without express permission from your hostess.

Pleasant Conversation

IF others persuade you to join in conversation that causes you to feel uncomfortable or that is totally inappropriate and distasteful, gracefully excuse yourself or politely suggest changing the subject, keeping the conversation light and cheerful. Never create an unwanted scene. Avoid imposing political or religious convictions on others, as these subjects tend to stir up heated discussions. Do not monopolize a conversation or hold anyone hostage with constant chatter. Allow others a chance to talk and visit.

Compliments and Requests

AT the party, be certain (once again) to express your appreciation for the invitation. Be complimentary about the house, the tea table, the party itself, or all three. Your hostess will truly appreciate a compliment for all the efforts.

IT is quite permissible to request an extra cup of tea, milk, sugar, a glass of water, or even an extra roll of tissue paper for the bathroom, but do not make any demands or request anything out of the ordinary, other than what your hostess has offered you. If you have any dietary restrictions, this should be discussed with your hostess upon responding to the invitation. If foods or beverages are not to your liking, avoid making any negative comments. Be a gracious guest.

Departures and Thank Yous

IF you know you need to depart before the party is over, notify your hostess of this in advance so that she will be aware of the time. If the party is in full swing when you have to excuse yourself, advise your hostess (quietly) that it is time for you to leave; then say goodbye to other guests. On the other hand, if you are the last guest to leave, do not overstay your welcome.

THANK your hostess again as you leave the party, and follow up with a personal thank you note within 2-3 days of the party.

Taking Tea and Refreshments

MOST teatime delicacies are meant to be finger foods. In other words, it is quite acceptable to use your fingers to pick up miniature sweets and savories. There are exceptions, however, when eating certain pastries, cakes, and scones which may require the use of a fork or a spoon. A hostess should make eating utensils available to all guests.

SCONES will require the use of a spreader for jam and clotted cream. When handling scones there are a couple of ways in which you may eat them, both of which are acceptable.

FIRST of all, place a small amount of jam and cream to the side of your plate before you begin spreading anything on your scone. Jam and/or lemon curd should be spread on your scone before the cream. The cream is always on top. Using a knife, slice the scone in half. With your knife, spread the jam and cream on one half of your scone. In this case a fork will be necessary to eat the scone. After you have finished your first half, repeat same by spreading jam and cream on the second half. Do not eat a scone like a sandwich. You may, however, use your fingers, by breaking off a little piece of the scone into a bite-sized piece. Use your knife to spread a small amount of jam and cream onto the piece of the scone and begin eating using your fingers. Continue breaking the scone apart into bite-sized pieces, one at a time, using the same method as before. In this case the use of a fork is not necessary.

PASTRIES and cakes may require the use of a fork or pastry spoon when frostings or cream fillings make it messy to pick them up using your fingers.

Serving Tea

WHEN adding milk, sugar cubes, granulated sugar, raw sugar, liquid sugar, or lemon slices to tea, there are a few simple rules you should follow. Hot tea should be poured into the cup before adding granulated sugar, raw sugar, sweeteners, or milk to your tea. A sugar spoon is used to transfer loose sugars from the sugar bowl into the cup. Stir tea with your own teaspoon. If sugar cubes are offered, a sugar tong is used to place a lump or two of cubed sugar into the bottom of the teacup before tea is poured into the cup. This will avoid splashing hot tea on you or the saucer. Putting milk in after the tea is poured gages the correct amount desired. Gently stir tea in a back and forth motion or gently swirl the tea around in your teacup to avoid making clanking noises. Lemon slices (never lemon wedges) should be placed gently in the tea after it is poured into your cup, allowing it to float on top of the tea. When pouring a second cup of tea, remove used lemon slice, adding a new slice for each cup of tea poured. Sip tea quietly; do not slurp. Place used teaspoon on saucer. There is no need to extend your pinky finger when drinking tea unless you feel the need to do so.

ICED TEA should be poured over ice in your glass. Add extra ice cubes to the glass when needed. If iced tea requires sweetening, add sugars or liquid sugar to the glass after the iced tea has been poured. When using liquid sugar, keep in mind that it is concentrated and requires very little to sweeten iced tea. Lemon slices or lemon wedges may be used for iced tea. Mint sprigs are also a nice touch, adding color and flavor. Use a small plate underneath the iced tea glass to contain moisture caused by sweating. This also gives you a place to rest your iced teaspoon when you are finished stirring.

Proper Attire

ONE of the first questions I am asked when conducting a tea seminar or tea presentation is usually a guarantee: What does one wear to afternoon tea? Because our present society is based on comfort and relaxation, this is no excuse to overlook the need to be neatly groomed or well dressed for afternoon tea. It is customary and considered fashionable to wear a dress or a skirt with a jacket, blouse, or sweater when attending or hosting an afternoon tea. However, dress slacks or business suits with slacks are also permissible for women. Jeans or outdoor clothing (including athletic shoes) are not considered proper attire for this occasion. Hats and gloves are no longer required in most social circles these days but many women love to use afternoon tea as an excuse to sport these accessories, especially when the invitation indicates a garden tea or a mother/daughter tea. A hostess may even request specific attire on the invitation itself.

THE Red Hat Societies have established a unique dress code over the past decade or so and can easily be identified when wearing red hats and purple outfits. I have witnessed just about everything from red sequined baseball caps and feathered boas to beautiful millinery creations and very chic designer outfits. It is a matter of personal taste and humor, in some cases. These spunky and lively ladies have nonetheless added color and sparkle to afternoon teas.

COURSE ONE

RECIPES FOR TEA SANDWICHES AND SPREADS

"To get into *best* society nowadays, one has either to
feed people, amuse people, or shock people."

OSCAR WILDE

THE IMPORTANCE OF BEING EARNEST

LITTLE crustless sandwiches are synonymous with afternoon tea. Thinly sliced cucumbers on white bread, flavored merely with fresh dill, butter, or cream cheese are usually offered no matter where you choose to take tea. Other savories such as miniature quiches, phyllo cups stuffed with fillings, petite biscuits, tiny croissants, as well as crackers topped with various meats or cheeses are also indicative of teatime delicacies. My advice is to create mini versions of your own favorite sandwich combinations. The possibilities are endless.

TEA sandwiches may be made in advance as long as they are securely wrapped and covered. Place them in airtight containers or on platters, covering sandwiches with a dampened tea towel or a dampened paper towel before sealing or securing them with plastic wrap. This will prevent breads from becoming dry and hardened. There is nothing worse than biting into a sandwich that appears to be stale. Protecting the sandwiches until they are ready to be presented is very important. I prefer simple, fresh, and tasty sandwiches over ones that are fancy, tasteless, and dry.

SANDWICH fillings and spreads may be made as early as the day before a party, but to ensure freshness, do not assemble them until the morning of the party. Use thinly sliced breads if possible. If your breads are too thick, gently roll over each slice with a rolling pin to slightly flatten the bread. Always spread a thin layer of butter or cream cheese on sandwiches before adding fillings or placing cucumbers and meats between the bread. This will prevent fillings from seeping through the bread and becoming soggy. Bring spreads or fillings to the very edges of the bread. Cut the crusts off after the sandwiches are made and cut into triangles or rectangles.

WHEN using cookie cutters to create different shapes for sandwiches, cut the bread into shapes first and then spread and add fillings to the ends of the bread. There are many types of bread to choose from but I am particularly partial to Pepperidge Farm breads because they offer a specific "thin" loaf which is available in both wheat and white and is very conducive to creating dainty teatime sandwiches.

WHEN making traditional tea sandwiches, one of my favorite ways for presenting and serving them is to cut the bread in triangular shapes (after crust is removed) by cutting on the diagonal of the sandwich in an X pattern, creating four equal triangles. Sandwiches may then be stacked side-by-side with points sticking up. Not only does this help the sandwiches maintain their moisture a bit longer, but the different colors of each filling show nicely. All that is needed for garnish is a very light sprinkling of finely chopped parsley, dill, or chives. I discovered this way of presenting tea sandwiches while enjoying afternoon tea at Harrods of London. I have to admit that I was expecting a much fancier presentation from Harrods, but the understated elegance and freshness were impressive.

COURSE ONE

These recipes are listed in the following pages

❦

Yam Biscuits

Shrimp Spread

Cheese Spread

Veggie Cream Cheese Spread

Cucumber Sandwiches

Fresh Tomato, Basil & Mozzarella Cheese Sandwiches

Italian Tea Sandwiches

Roast Beef Sandwiches

Ham & Cheese Sandwiches

Salmon Sandwiches

Chicken Salad

Ham Salad

Egg Salad

Tuna Salad

❦

BASIC TEA SANDWICH COMBINATIONS

The following tea sandwiches are some of my favorites:

Cucumber *on white bread with butter and dill or vegetable cream cheese or shrimp spread*

Egg Salad *on white bread with butter*

Tuna Salad *on white or wheat bread with butter and dill*

Chicken Salad *on white bread, wheat bread, or mini croissant with butter*

Ham Salad or Ham & Cheese *on white or rye bread or mini yam biscuits with butter*

Mini Yam Biscuits *with butter or mustards*

Roast Beef with Fried Onions *on white or pumpernickel bread with horseradish sauce*

Fresh Tomatoes, Mozzarella Cheese, and Basil Leaves *on white bread with butter*

Salmon *on pumpernickel with plain or veggie cream cheese or shrimp spread*

YAM BISCUITS

While on a buying trip to Dallas, Texas in 1988, a lovely southern woman
shared this recipe with me. She had catered an event at one of the many
showrooms for the semi-annual gift show and filled her yam biscuits
with thinly sliced ham and various cheeses.
I have also served these biscuits with ham salad.

❧

2 ½ cups SELF-RISING flour
(Add ¼ cup more flour, if needed)
¾ cup finely chopped pecans
¾ cup milk
1-cup cooked yams or sweet potatoes
¾ cup melted butter

❧

Preheat oven to 350 degrees.
Beat yams or sweet potatoes until smooth and creamy.
Add melted butter and milk and beat again until smooth texture.
By hand, add 2 ½ cups of SELF-RISING flour with the
chopped pecans and knead together until it's a bread-like consistency.
Add a little more flour, if necessary, until hands don't stick to dough.
On a floured surface, roll the dough out to about ½" thick.
Use a small round cookie cutter to cut dough.
Place biscuits on slightly greased baking sheets 2"-3" apart.

Bake for 10-15 minutes or until biscuits are lightly browned.
Let cool completely before storing in an airtight container or freeze them.

SHRIMP SPREAD

1 small can broken deveined shrimp

8 oz. cream cheese, softened

3-4 green onions (with stems) chopped

¼ teaspoon lemon juice

¼ cup mayonnaise

Drain the shrimp and rinse in cold water. Set aside.
With an electric mixer, beat softened cream cheese with
mayonnaise and lemon juice for 10-15 minutes until light and fluffy.
Add chopped green onions and shrimp to cream cheese mixture.
Mix well until all ingredients are blended.
Refrigerate overnight in an airtight container.
Pipe onto bread rounds or use as a spread on tea sandwiches
with cucumber or salmon.

CHEESE SPREAD

1 jar KRAFT Old English Cheese Spread

1 jar KRAFT Bleu Cheese Spread

3 oz. cream cheese, softened

⅛ teaspoon garlic powder

Beat cheeses together for several minutes until light and fluffy.
Mix in garlic powder and beat again. Cover and refrigerate for at least 2 hours.
Bring to room temperature before using.

VEGGIE CREAM CHEESE SPREAD

2 – 8 oz. cream cheese, softened

One box dry vegetable soup mix

Beat cream cheese several minutes until light and fluffy.
Stir in dry vegetable soup mix.
Cover and refrigerate for at least 2 hours.
Bring to room temperature before using.

CUCUMBER SANDWICHES

When making cucumber sandwiches, peel and slice cucumbers thin.
Place in single layers on top of paper towels and cover with paper towels, removing
moisture well before making sandwiches. Cucumbers should be crunchy, not soggy.
Spread a thin layer of butter or cream cheese on both sides of bread.
Place cucumbers on one slice, cover and cut.

FRESH TOMATO, BASIL AND
MOZZARELLA CHEESE SANDWICHES

When making these sandwiches, use fresh, ripe tomatoes, sliced thin.
Slice fresh mozzarella cheese thin. Rinse and pat dry fresh whole basil leaves.
Butter both sides of bread and layer with fresh tomatoes, cheese and basil leaves.
Or serve open face on one slice of cut, round bread.

ITALIAN TEA SANDWICHES

Thinly sliced salami, Italian ham and provolone cheese pair well with thinly sliced
Italian white bread, lightly buttered and then spread with a little Italian Dressing.

Italian Dressing: *(Shake vigorously before using)*

½ cup Extra Virgin Olive Oil

½ teaspoon dried oregano

½ teaspoon lemon juice

½ teaspoon garlic powder

1 Tablespoon grated Parmesan cheese

ROAST BEEF AND FRIED ONION SANDWICHES

Use ready-prepared fried onions, any good brand will do.
When making these sandwiches, lightly butter both sides of bread.
Spread a thin layer of horseradish sauce on both sides of bread.
Place medium-rare slices of roast beef on one side of bread.
Top roast beef with some baked fried onions.
Cover with other slice of bread before cutting.

HAM AND CHEESE SANDWICHES

Use any quality baked ham with any favorite cheese.
Pair Swiss, Munster, Cheddar, Monterey Jack, or American
with any mustard or mayonnaise of choice.

SALMON SANDWICHES

You may use fresh, thinly sliced salmon atop any favorite spread or bread.
To make salmon spread:
beat an 8 ounce brick of softened cream cheese until light and fluffy.
Add one 6 ounce can skinless, boneless salmon filet, drained.
Add drained, flaked salmon to cream cheese with 1/2 teaspoon lemon juice.
Beat until blended. Cover and refrigerate until ready to use.
This spread is also great on pumpernickel bread.

CHICKEN SALAD

There are endless variations of chicken salad recipes. This one is especially good and creamy.
Dried apricots are difficult to cut through a closed sandwich. You may prefer to use the chopped,
dried apricots when making mini croissant sandwiches, open-face sandwiches, or atop lettuce leaves.

3 cups cooked chicken, diced
1 ½ cups celery hearts, thinly sliced
3 teaspoons lemon juice
1 cup mayonnaise
¼ cup sour cream
1 teaspoon salt
½ teaspoon white ground pepper
1 teaspoon dry mustard
1 cup seedless green or red grapes cut in quarters, optional
¼ cup chopped dried apricots, optional
¾ cup toasted slivered almonds, optional

Combine: lemon juice, mayonnaise, sour cream, salt, pepper and dry mustard together.
Add chicken and sliced celery together and toss gently with mayonnaise mixture.
Stir in grapes, dried apricots and slivered almonds if you so desire.

HAM SALAD

Ham freezes well, so next time you have left-over ham from a holiday or
special dinner, make a homemade ham salad to use up the leftovers.

2 cups finely chopped, cooked ham
½ cup finely diced celery
1 teaspoon grated onion
⅓ cup mayonnaise
1 teaspoon prepared mustard
1 Tablespoon sweet relish

Combine together: ham, celery, onion, mayonnaise, mustard, and sweet relish
Refrigerate until ready to serve. You may pulse this salad a couple
of times in a food processor to make it more spreadable.

EGG SALAD

I prefer a simple egg salad recipe. However, adding a creamy ranch-style dressing
along with mayonnaise or a bit of curry powder, offers an added dash of flavor.

6 hard boiled eggs, peeled and chopped fine
½ cup mayonnaise
½ teaspoon salt
¼ teaspoon white pepper
¼ teaspoon celery salt

After eggs are chopped, mix gently with your favorite salad dressing.
Fold in salt, pepper and celery salt.
Refrigerate until ready to make into sandwiches.
*Note: You may use ¼ cup salad dressing and ¼ cup Ranch-style dressing for a tangier flavor.
If you prefer your egg salad more moist, add 2 Tablespoons extra of salad dressing.*

TUNA SALAD

2 – 6 ounce cans white tuna in water, drained and chopped
* ½ cup mayonnaise
¼ teaspoon salt
¼ teaspoon black pepper
1 teaspoon yellow mustard
1 Tablespoon sweet relish
½ cup thinly chopped celery

Drain tuna, chop, and set aside. Mix mayonnaise, salt, pepper, mustard, and sweet relish together.
Add chopped celery and tuna to mayonnaise mixture. Refrigerate until ready to use.
*Add more mayonnaise if you prefer a creamier texture.

BASIC SCONES, RECIPE ON PAGE 64

COURSE TWO
RECIPES FOR SCONES, SHORTBREAD & TEA BREADS

"My hour for *tea* is half-past five,
and my buttered toast *waits* for nobody."

WILKIE COLLINS
THE WOMAN IN WHITE

NOTHING speaks teatime more than freshly baked scones, slathered with strawberry jam, and topped with cream. There are two secrets, however, to making great scones:

1. Mix ingredients together with as little handling or kneading as possible.

2. Use only the freshest ingredients possible.

IT is that simple! Once you have mastered the task of creating melt-in-your-mouth scones, every other teatime temptation is merely incidental. A warm, moist scone is the ultimate indulgence and most satisfying comfort food you can serve your guests.

FOR years, I thought waiting to mix scone batter together moments before popping them into the oven would result in fresher-tasting scones. I was wrong. I discovered that scones still maintain moisture and freshness when mixing, cutting, and refrigerating the dough long before baking them. (However, I usually do not make my dough earlier than the evening before or the morning of my party.) Placing the pre-cut scones on baking sheets, tightly wrapped and refrigerated for several hours, allows the flavors to set while eliminating the mess of cleaning the kitchen again as guests begin arriving. After removing scones from the refrigerator, I do recommend letting them come to room temperature before baking. The aroma of scones baking in the oven is intoxicating!

COURSE TWO

These recipes are listed in the following pages

Basic Scones

Homemade Clotted Cream

Lemon or Lime Curd

Honey-Lemon Butter

Strawberry Butter

Chocolate Shortbread Cookies

English Shortbread

Cranberry Orange Bread

Chocolate Tea Bread

Date and Nut Bread

Banana Bread

Pumpkin Bread

Zucchini Bread

BASIC SCONES

This is the basic scone recipe I always use.

For added color and flavor, use dried fruits such as chopped apricots, cranberries,
raisins, or currents. Chocolate chips may also be used in this recipe.
Grated lemon or orange zest adds wonderful flavor. If you prefer cinnamon scones, use a sprinkling
of cinnamon and sugar atop scones after brushing milk or egg wash on top just prior to
baking. Scones are lighter and fluffier when incorporating skim milk into the batter.
The heavier the milk or cream used, the denser these scones will become.

❧

2 cups all-purpose flour

6 Tablespoons butter

¼ cup granulated sugar

½ cup milk or cream

1 Tablespoon baking powder

1 egg

½ teaspoon salt

½ cup chopped dried fruit, optional

❧

Preheat oven to 425 degrees. Sift dry ingredients together.

Cut butter into dry mixture with a pastry cutter or fork.
Whisk milk and egg together with a fork and add to dry ingredients.
Using the fork, stir together until just blended.
Add dried fruit, zest, and/or chocolate chips if you desire.
Flour counter surface and lightly knead dough until just blended.
Pat dough into a 6" – 7" circle, about ½" thick.
Cut into 8 wedges OR cut dough into shapes, using a 2" – 3" cookie cutter.
Place on cookie sheet.
You may brush milk OR egg wash on top of scones
and sprinkle a little sugar on top before baking.
Bake for about 10 minutes.
Remove from oven when scones are golden on top.
Serve warm with jam, lemon curd, and clotted cream.

HOMEMADE CLOTTED CREAM

1 cup heavy whipping cream
¼ cup powdered sugar
1 cup sour cream

Beat cream until soft peaks begin to form.
Add powdered sugar and continue beating until cream is firm.
Fold in sour cream. Refrigerate.
Serve with warm scones, tea breads or any type of fresh fruit.

LEMON OR LIME CURD

Lemon curd is traditionally served at teatime
but I find lime curd is just as delicious!

Grated peel of 4 lemons OR 4 limes
Juice of 4 lemons OR 4 limes (about 1 cup)
4 eggs, beaten at room temperature
½ cup butter, cut into small pieces
2 cups granulated sugar

In the top of a double boiler, combine
lemon/lime peel, lemon/lime juice, eggs, butter, and sugar.
Place over simmering water and stir until sugar is dissolved.
Continue to cook, stirring frequently, until thickened and smooth.
Let cool and refrigerate.
These flavored curds are delicious with warm scones and clotted cream
but may also be used in pre-baked phyllo cups as a dessert.
With a squiggle of whipped cream and a piece of candied fruit atop,
the cream presents an outstanding-looking pastry.
A tiny mint leaf also looks attractive on top of the cream.

HONEY-LEMON BUTTER

My friend, Mary Peters, owned and operated The Candlewick Inn
in Williamsburg, Virginia for over 20 years and shared these
flavored butter recipes with me.
These butters are delicious on scones and tea breads.

❧

1 stick butter, room temperature
¼ cup honey
2 Tablespoons fresh lemon juice
1 Tablespoon grated lemon peel

❧

Mix all ingredients together, beating until smooth and creamy.
Cover and refrigerate.
Bring to room temperature before serving.

✦

STRAWBERRY BUTTER

❧

½ stick butter, room temperature
1 ¼ cups powdered sugar
¼ cup fresh strawberries, crushed
½ teaspoon vanilla
a pinch of salt

❧

Beat together butter and sugar.
Add vanilla and salt and beat again.
Stir in crushed strawberries.
Cover and refrigerate for at least two hours.
Bring to room temperature before serving.

CHOCOLATE SHORTBREAD COOKIES

This recipe is outstanding and so easy to make. If stored in an airtight container or tin,
these chocolate shortbread cookies will remain fresh for a week.

⁓❧⁓

1 stick butter
¾ cup granulated sugar
⅓ cup unsweetened cocoa powder
1 egg
1 Tablespoon whole milk or cream
1 teaspoon vanilla
2 cups flour
¼ teaspoon salt

⁓❧⁓

Beat butter with an electric mixer until light and fluffy.
Mix sugar and unsweetened cocoa powder together.
Slowly add sugar and cocoa mixture to butter, beating on low speed.
Beat in egg, cream and vanilla.
In a separate bowl, mix flour with salt.
Slowly add flour and salt to mixture, stirring until blended.
Sprinkle some powdered sugar on counter
and pat dough evenly to ½ inch thickness.
Lightly roll over dough with a rolling pin to smooth dough.
Dip a cookie cutter into some granulated or powdered sugar and cut dough.
Place shortbread shapes 2" apart onto a Silpat or slightly greased cookie sheet.
Bake at 350 degrees for 10 minutes or until set.
Cool completely on wire racks.
Sprinkle lightly with powdered sugar before serving.

HELPFUL HINTS

Silicone pads or liners work great on cookie sheets
when baking cookies and scones.

ENGLISH SHORTBREAD

Shortbread may be made well in advance of any party.
In fact, shortbread, like pound cake, is almost better the second or third day,
as the rich, buttery flavor has a chance to set in.

꒰꒱

2 cups all-purpose flour
1 cup cornstarch
pinch of salt
1 cup butter, softened
*1 cup superfine sugar
1 Tablespoon granulated sugar for top

꒰꒱

Sift flour, cornstarch, and salt into a bowl and set aside.
In another bowl, cream butter with sugar.
Beat well until light and fluffy.
With a wooden spoon, gradually work in dry ingredients.
Press dough into an ungreased 8 X 8 inch baking pan.
Prick surface all over with a fork.
Using a sharp knife, lightly score surface into 20 squares.
Sprinkle with 1 Tablespoon granulated sugar before baking.
Bake at 325 degrees for about 40 minutes or until golden.

DO NOT LET THEM BROWN!

Cool completely in pan. To serve, follow the score lines and cut into little squares.

*To make superfine sugar, just place granulated sugar in a
food processor or blender and pulse or blend
until sugar is superfine.

CRANBERRY ORANGE BREAD

This is one of my very favorite tea breads. It is especially good
around holiday time with a good cup of holiday spiced tea!

⋯

2 cups all-purpose flour
1 ½ teaspoons baking powder
½ teaspoon baking soda
½ teaspoon salt
1 cup granulated sugar
2 cups fresh cranberries, sliced in half
Grated zest and juice of 1 orange
¼ cup melted butter
1 egg, beaten
½ cup finely chopped pecans or walnuts, optional

⋯

Combine flour, baking powder, salt, sugar, nuts, and sliced cranberries.
With a wooden spoon, gently mix ingredients until blended.
Combine the orange zest, juice, and melted butter
with enough water to make ¾ cup.
Beat in the egg. Pour wet mixture over dry ingredients
and gently stir until all ingredients are moist.
Spoon batter into a greased and floured 9 x 5 inch loaf pan or small loaf pans.
Bake at 350 degrees for about 60 to 70 minutes, or until
a wooden pick or cake tester inserted in center comes out clean.
Reduce baking time if using small pans.
Cool completely on wire rack.

CHOCOLATE TEA BREAD

My friend, Vicki, shared this recipe with me and
I feel it is one of the best tea breads ever!
The applesauce in this recipe keeps bread extra moist.

❦

½ cup applesauce
⅓ cup shortening
2 eggs
⅓ cup water
1 ¼ cups granulated sugar
1 ¼ cups all-purpose flour
⅓ cup baking cocoa
1 teaspoon baking soda
¾ teaspoon salt
¼ teaspoon baking powder
1 cup semisweet mini chocolate chips
⅓ cup chopped walnuts, optional

❦

In a mixing bowl, combine:
applesauce, shortening, eggs, water, and sugar.
Beat on low speed for 30 seconds.
Combine dry ingredients and add to mixture.
Beat on low for 30 more seconds.
Beat on high for 2 1/2 minutes, scraping bowl occasionally.
Fold in chocolate chips and nuts.
Pour into a greased and floured 9 x 5 x 3 inch loaf pan,
or smaller if you wish.
Bake at 350 degrees for 60-70 minutes
or until a toothpick inserted in the center comes out clean.
Cool in pan 15 minutes before removing to a wire rack to cool completely.

DATE AND NUT BREAD

This is another one of those classic, fool-proof recipes.

2 cups boiled water

1 cup chopped dates

Soak chopped dates in the 2 cups boiled water and set aside.

½ cup butter, softened

2 cups sugar

2 eggs

2 teaspoons baking soda

4 cups all-purpose flour

1 cup chopped nuts

1 teaspoon vanilla

Beat butter and sugar together until light and fluffy.
Add the eggs, one at a time.
Mix dry ingredients together and set aside.
Add cooled dates with the water to the creamed mixture.
Then add all of the dry ingredients and mix well.
Add vanilla and lastly, stir in nuts.
Grease and flour 4 small or
2 medium sized baking loaf pans.
Pour batter evenly into pans, filling ⅔ full.
Bake at 350 degrees for 1 hour.
Make only 1 recipe at a time.

HELPFUL HINTS

When making tea breads for afternoon tea trays, try using smaller
loaf pans for more petite-like slices. The baking time will usually
be diminished by 10-20 minutes when using smaller baking pans.

BANANA BREAD

This recipe has been in my family for as long as I can remember.
It doesn't require a lot of ingredients but remains
the best banana bread I have ever eaten!

❧

½ cup butter, room temperature
1-cup sugar
2 eggs
3 ripe bananas, mashed
2-cups all-purpose flour
1-teaspoon baking soda
¼ teaspoon salt

❧

Beat butter well, adding sugar slowly until light and fluffy.
Beat in eggs, one at a time.
Mash bananas with a fork and stir them into the batter.
Add dry ingredients and stir into the mixture.
Grease and flour 3 small bread pans or 1 large bread pan.
Bake at 350 degrees for 45-60 minutes or until lightly browned on top
or when cake tester inserted in center comes out clean.
Let cool in pan for 5 minutes before removing to a wire rack.
Serve warm with butter, cream cheese, or clotted cream.

PUMPKIN BREAD

This bread is great any time of year
but is especially decadent during fall and winter.

❧

15 oz. can pumpkin
1 cup vegetable oil
$\frac{2}{3}$ cup water
4 large eggs
3 cups granulated sugar
3 $\frac{1}{3}$ cups flour
2 teaspoons baking soda
1 teaspoon ground cinnamon
1 teaspoon ground nutmeg
$\frac{1}{8}$ teaspoon ground cloves
$\frac{1}{2}$ cup raisins, optional

❧

Mix canned pumpkin, vegetable oil, water, and eggs together,
beating until creamy. Add sugar and beat again.
Mix remaining dry ingredients together and blend until creamy.
Grease and flour 2 large OR 4 medium OR 8 small loaf pans.
Bake bread at 350 degrees for 45-60 minutes,
depending upon the size of your pans.

ZUCCHINI BREAD

You may add chocolate chips to this zucchini bread for added flavor!

❧❦❧

3 eggs

1 cup light oil

2 cups granulated sugar

2 teaspoons vanilla extract

2 cups (shredded) zucchini, unpeeled

8 ½ oz. can crushed pineapple, well drained

3 cups all-purpose flour

2 teaspoons baking soda

1 ½ teaspoons cinnamon

1 teaspoon salt

¾ teaspoon nutmeg

¼ teaspoon baking powder

1 cup chopped, pitted dates

1 cup finely chopped nuts, optional

❧❦❧

Sift all dry ingredients together and set aside.

Beat eggs well; add oil; then sugar and vanilla, beating until thick.

Add dates and nuts and mix well.

Add dry ingredients and blend until just mixed altogether.

Grease and flour 2 medium or 4 small loaf pans.

Bake at 350 degrees for approximately one hour or until golden brown.

LEMON SQUARES, RECIPE ON PAGE 98

COURSE THREE

RECIPES FOR COOKIES, PASTRIES & CAKES

"Life is uncertain, eat *dessert* first!"

-ANONYMOUS

PASTRIES, cakes, tarts, and cookies are acceptable excuses for extreme indulgence. Not only do I crave sweets but I am a confirmed and hopeless chocoholic and truly believe no tea party is complete without offering at least one extraordinary chocolate dessert to guests. Who can resist the temptation of a chocolate dipped strawberry to set afternoon tea in motion? Desserts may be offered as the grand finale or perhaps the perfect beginning to afternoon tea! Either way, offer your guests a variety of colors and textures when assembling dessert trays.

IF sweets crowd the top tier of your tea server, use additional serving pieces, displaying your desserts in appealing ways. Miniature cakes look fabulous atop a small pedestal cake dish or on wide candle holders, or select a special platter to acknowledge one outstanding dessert. However you choose to present them, afternoon tea cakes are traditionally offered in small slices or bite-size pieces. It is definitely more time consuming baking and creating miniature desserts, but tea time is definitely worthy of these efforts.

SOME bake-ware manufacturers produce a variety of mini baking pans for round cakes, angel food cakes, Bundt cakes, spring form pans, and breads. Over the years I have collected an assortment of all these items mentioned. However, small bake ware pans and molds are not always easy to find. I suggest making the investment when you happen upon them while antiquing or shopping gourmet cooking stores and catalogs.

COURSE THREE

These recipes are listed in the following pages

❧

Cream Filled Strawberries

Double Dipped Chocolate Strawberries

Aunt Etta's Butter Cookies

Apricot Crescent Cookies

Double Chocolate Chip Cookies

Ice Box Oatmeal Cookies

Lemon Drop Cookies

Russian Tea Cookies

Raspberry Jam Cookies

Chocolate Lady Fingers

Frosted Cake Brownies & Chocolate Frosting

Traditional English Trifle

Lemon Cheese Bars

Lemon Squares

Carrot Cake & Cream Cheese Frosting

Chocolate Pound Cake

Strawberry Angel Food Cream Cake

Two Tone Cheese Cake

Sour Cream Pound Cake

Fresh Flower Cake (non-edible)

CREAM FILLED STRAWBERRIES

These cream filled strawberries look fabulous served on a silver tray,
surrounded by dark green, waxy leaves.

❧

18 Jumbo strawberries, room temperature

1 cup heavy cream, whipped

4 oz. package Vanilla INSTANT pudding

1 cup milk

1 teaspoon almond extract

❧

Cut stems off strawberries and set strawberry with point facing up.
With a sharp knife, cut a deep X in top of each berry.
With fingertip, gently separate each berry apart to make room for filling.
Set aside.
In a large bowl, with a wire whisk or an electric mixer,
prepare pudding as directed on label but use only 1 cup of milk.
With a rubber spatula, gently fold whipped cream
and almond extract into prepared pudding.
Spoon or pipe cream mixture into berries.
Cover and refrigerate until ready to serve.

DOUBLE DIPPED CHOCOLATE STRAWBERRIES

I love serving chocolate dipped strawberries at teatime.
Use only fresh, red-ripened berries. Make certain strawberries are
completely dry and at room temperature before dipping.

❧

12 oz. of semisweet or milk chocolate quality melting chocolate
12 oz. of white quality melting chocolate
1 quart of fresh strawberries with stems, rinsed and completely dried

❧

Melt white chocolate first, separately from semisweet or milk chocolate
by placing in a pan over simmering water, stirring until completely melted; or
place chocolate in a microwave safe bowl and set time at 15 second intervals,
stirring between times until chocolate is completely melted.
Don't overheat chocolate.

Holding each strawberry by the stem,
carefully dip each berry into the white chocolate,
leaving about 1/4 inch of the red berry showing.
Place each white chocolate dipped berry on waxed paper to dry

Meanwhile, in a separate bowl, melt the semisweet or milk chocolate
the same way you did the white chocolate.
Holding each strawberry by the stem, carefully dip the
white chocolate covered berries in the semisweet or milk chocolate,
leaving about 1/4 inch of the white chocolate showing.
Again, place the chocolate dipped berries back on the waxed paper to dry.

It's best to dip strawberries the day you intend to eat them otherwise the juice
from the berries has a tendency to separate the berry from the chocolate.
Serve chocolate dipped strawberries at room temperature.

AUNT ETTA'S BUTTER COOKIES

This recipe was handed down by my great aunt, Henrietta Davidson-Brabon.
Aunt Etta believed the two secrets to making these delicious butter cookies is the use
of heavy cream vs. milk and watching carefully so as not to let the cookies brown,
by baking them one sheet at a time in the center of your oven.
These butter cookies melt in your mouth!

1 cup butter
1 ½ cups granulated sugar
Pinch of salt
2 eggs, room temperature
1 teaspoon vanilla extract
3 Tablespoons heavy cream
3 cups all-purpose flour

Beat butter until smooth and creamy.
Add sugar slowly; then salt.
Add eggs, one at a time, beating well after each addition.
Add dry ingredients, alternately with cream.
Lastly, add vanilla extract.

Put the cookie dough through a butter form cookie press.
Press cookies onto an ungreased cookie sheet.
Make certain the dough is stiff enough to leave lines in the cookies.
Bake one sheet at a time in a 375 degree oven for about 8 minutes.

Do not let cookies brown. Cool completely on wire racks.

APRICOT CRESCENT COOKIES

I served these cookies in my teashop and they were always a hit. Because the apricot jam tends to
ooze out of the dough when baking, I find it necessary to use a Silpat or silicone
sheet when baking these to eliminate a burnt mess on the cookie sheet afterwards.

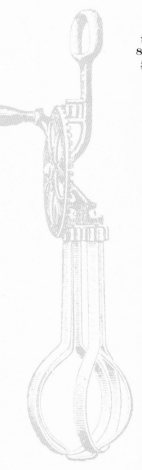

1 cup butter
2 cups all-purpose flour
1 egg yolk, beaten
½ cup sour cream
½ cup apricot preserves
½ cup flaked coconut
¼ cup finely chopped pecans
Powdered sugar

Cut butter into flour with a pastry cutter until mixture resembles coarse meal.
Combine egg yolk and sour cream. Stir into flour mixture.
Divide and shape dough into 4 balls.
Wrap each portion of dough in waxed paper and chill for 4 hours.
Roll out one portion of dough on a floured surface to a 10" circle.
Keep remaining dough chilled until ready to roll.
Spread 2 Tablespoons of apricot preserves on each circle and sprinkle with
2 Tablespoons of coconut and 1 Tablespoon of pecans.
Cut each circle into 12 wedges; roll up wedges, beginning at wide end.
Place point-side down on ungreased baking sheets.
Sprinkle lightly with granulated sugar.
Repeat procedure with remaining dough.
Bake at 350 degrees for 20 minutes or until lightly browned.
Remove from baking sheets and cool on wire racks.
Store in airtight container or freeze.

Sprinkle with powdered sugar before serving.

DOUBLE CHOCOLATE CHIP COOKIES
If you are going to make chocolate chip cookies, why not double your pleasure?

❧

Melt 6 oz. semisweet chocolate and set aside to cool
½ cup (1 stick) butter, room temperature
½ cup packed dark brown sugar
½ cup granulated sugar
1 egg
2 teaspoons vanilla
1 cup all purpose flour
½ teaspoon baking soda
Pinch of salt
6 oz. semisweet chocolate chips
½ cup chopped nuts, optional

❧

Preheat oven to 350 degrees.
Beat butter and sugars together until creamy.
Add egg and vanilla, beating again.
Add melted chocolate, beating until just mixed.
Add dry ingredients.
Stir in chocolate chips and chopped nuts.
Drop batter by rounded teaspoons 2" apart onto ungreased baking sheet.
Bake 10 minutes.
Cool on sheets for 5 minutes before transferring to wire rack. Cool completely.

ICE BOX OATMEAL COOKIES

My mother-in-law shared this recipe with me many years ago.
These cookies are very light and crispy and pair
well with iced tea or lemonade.
I regard this recipe as a summertime treat.

1 cup butter
1 cup powdered sugar
2 teaspoons vanilla extract
1 ½ cups all-purpose flour
½ teaspoon baking soda
1 cup quick-rolling oatmeal

Preheat oven to 350 degrees.
Beat butter and powdered sugar together for several minutes.
Add vanilla, and other dry ingredients.
Mix until well blended.
Divide dough in half and make 2 long narrow rolls.
Wrap in plastic wrap and refrigerate overnight.
Lightly grease cookie sheets.
Unwrap cookie dough and cut into thin round cookies.
Place on cookie sheets. Bake for 15 minutes.
Let cool and sprinkle lightly with powdered sugar.

LEMON DROP COOKIES
These cookies are especially good with a hot cup of Earl Grey tea!

❧

½ cup butter (1 stick)

⅔ cup granulated sugar

2 teaspoons grated lemon rind

1 egg

4 Tablespoons lemon juice

1 ¾ cups all-purpose flour

¼ teaspoon baking soda

¼ teaspoon cream of tartar

½ teaspoon salt

½ cup finely chopped nuts

Powdered sugar

❧

In a large bowl: beat butter and granulated sugar together until light and fluffy.
Add lemon rind and egg, beating well again. Stir in lemon juice.
Sift together flour, baking soda, cream of tartar, and salt.
Add to the creamed mixture, blending well. Stir in nuts.
Chill dough for at least 30 minutes.
Flour hands and form dough into small balls.
Place about an inch apart on an ungreased cookie sheet.
Bake at 350 degrees for 10-15 minutes.
Cool cookies completely before covering in powdered sugar.

RUSSIAN TEA COOKIES
I have tasted many pecan butter cookies but find this recipe to be the best!

❧

1 cup butter

½ cup powdered sugar

1 teaspoon vanilla

2 ¼ cups cake flour

¼ teaspoon salt

½ cup finely chopped pecans

Powdered sugar for rolling cookies

❧

Mix butter, ½ cup powdered sugar, and vanilla well.
Sift together flour, salt and chopped pecans.
Stir dry ingredients into butter mixture.
Chill at least one hour and form into 1 inch balls.
Place on ungreased cookie sheets, 2 inches apart.
Bake at 400 degrees for 10-12 minutes.
Cool cookies and roll in powdered sugar.
Store in an airtight container.

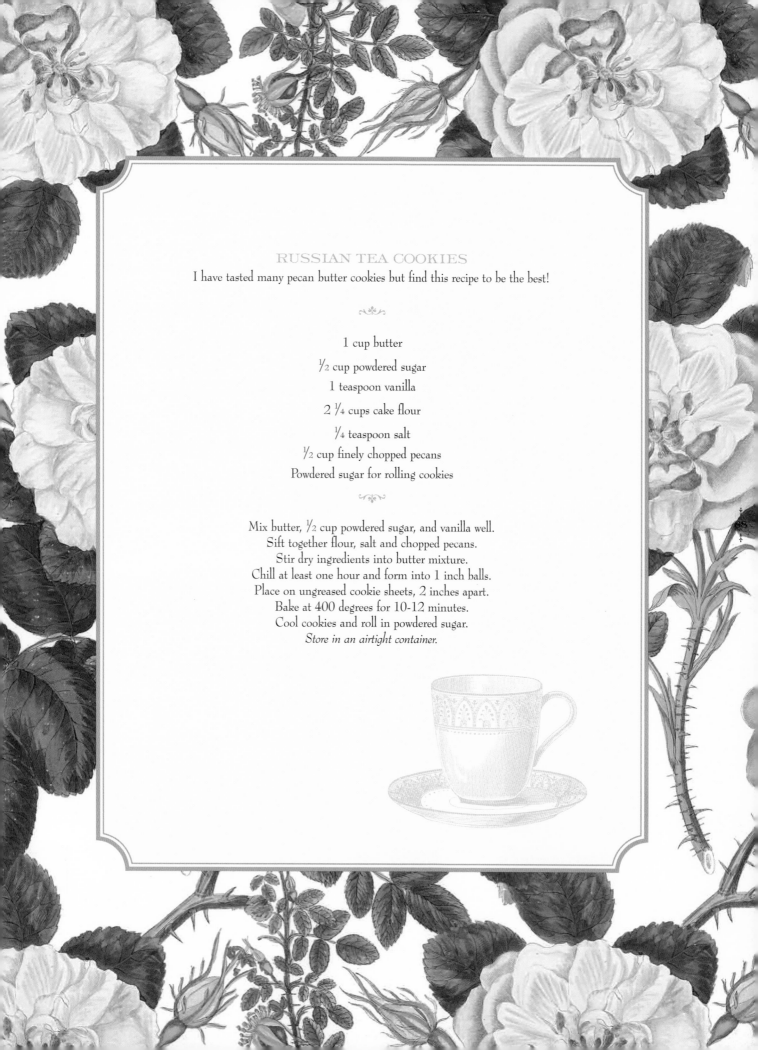

RASPBERRY JAM COOKIES

I always served these raspberry jam cookies in my teashop.
They are exceptionally light and buttery tasting.
The powdered sugar sprinkled on top sticks to the outer edges of the cookies,
but eventually melts into the center filling making them just a bit sweeter.

1 cup butter
½ cup granulated sugar
1 egg YOLK
½ teaspoon vanilla extract
2 ½ cups all-purpose flour
Raspberry jam

Preheat oven to 350 degrees.
Beat butter until creamy. Add sugar a little at a time.
Beat in egg yolk and vanilla.
Add flour and beat until just blended.
Roll dough into 1-inch balls. Place 2 inches apart on cookie sheet.
Indent centers with your thumb and pinch sides together to even out the dough.
Place a small amount of raspberry jam in center of each cookie.
Bake for 8-10 minutes. *Do not let the cookies brown.*
When removing from oven, leave cookies on sheets
for a few minutes before removing to a wire rack to cool completely.
Cookies will be very fragile.
Store cookies in an airtight container.
These cookies also freeze well.
Before serving, sprinkle with powdered sugar.

TOP: RASPBERRY JAM COOKIES

LEFT: APRICOT CRESCENT COOKIES · RIGHT: LEMON DROP COOKIES

CHOCOLATE LADY FINGERS

The filling for this recipe was in part from another recipe
that was quite popular about 30 years ago.
Used as a filling between lady fingers gives it a new look
for a delicate tea pastry.

❧

1 package of ladyfingers *(usually found in any bakery section)*
4 oz. cream cheese, softened
½ cup whipped topping or whipped cream
1/2 cup powdered sugar
1 ½ boxes INSTANT chocolate pudding
1 ¾ cups COLD milk
1 teaspoon vanilla extract

❧

Beat cream cheese until soft and fluffy.
Add whipped topping or whipping cream and powdered sugar
to cream cheese and beat until creamy. Set aside.
In a new mixing bowl, mix pudding with COLD milk and vanilla.
Beat together until thick and creamy.
Refrigerate pudding for at least an hour.
Take ladyfingers and open them.
Spread softened cream cheese mixture over bottoms of each ladyfinger.
Spread or pipe on a thick layer of chocolate pudding mixture
over the bottom lady finger.
Place tops of ladyfingers over pudding mixture.
Refrigerate.
Sprinkle with a light dusting of cocoa powder before serving.

FROSTED CAKE BROWNIES

This recipe has been in my family since my childhood.
These are not your traditional chewy brownies but a dense, rich chocolate cake.
My family voted this to be the best and most addictive recipe!
You can't eat just one.

❦

½ cup baking cocoa
½ cup boiled water
Boil water and stir in cocoa until smooth. Set aside to cool.

1 cup butter
2 cups sugar
4 eggs
2 cups all-purpose flour
½ cup milk or evaporated milk
1 teaspoon vanilla
1 cup chopped walnuts or pecans (optional)

❦

Preheat oven to 375 degrees.
While cocoa is cooling, beat butter until creamy.
Add sugar, a little at a time, and beat again until fluffy.
Add cooled cocoa mixture in small amounts and blend well.
Add eggs, one at a time and beat about 3 minutes.
Add flour, alternately with milk.
Add vanilla and stir in nuts, if desired.
Grease and flour a regular size jellyroll pan and pour batter into pan.
Bake for 20-25 minutes. Cool in pan on wire rack.
When completely cool, frost with chocolate butter cream frosting.
Cut into small squares and serve.

Top each frosted brownie square with a piping of fresh whipping cream
and cut a raspberry in half to top for an elegant presentation.

By adding a Tablespoon of brewed coffee to this frosting, creates a rich, glossy look to it.

10 Tablespoons butter, softened
¾ cup cocoa powder
¼ teaspoon salt
2 Tablespoons corn syrup
3 cups powdered sugar
4-5 Tablespoons whole milk or heavy cream, warmed

Using an electric mixer, beat butter, cocoa, corn syrup and salt
for several minutes until smooth and creamy.
On low speed, gradually beat in powdered sugar alternately with milk.
After that is incorporated, mix on high speed until light and fluffy.

NOTE: Add more powdered sugar if frosting is too loose.

Trifles can be made in a variety of ways using various substitutions

Chocolate cake with chocolate pudding and whipped cream
may be substituted for vanilla cake and pudding.
Adding fresh pineapple, bananas, fresh strawberries and chocolate sauce
can turn a classic English Trifle into an American favorite,
the banana split, by topping it with whipped cream, nuts & cherries.
Again, use your favorite fruits and fillings to create a recipe
to satisfy your own taste.

TRADITIONAL ENGLISH TRIFLE

❧

One pound cake

Sherry

Fresh, whole raspberries or fresh strawberries, hulled and sliced

2 boxes INSTANT French Vanilla Pudding

8 oz. container COOL WHIP

3 ½ cups COLD milk

1 cup heavy whipping cream, whipped

¼ cup powdered sugar

❧

Cut pound cake into slices and set aside.
Mix pudding with cold milk and beat until thick and creamy.
Fold in COOL WHIP and set aside.
Beat heavy cream until soft peaks form.
Sprinkle powdered sugar over cream and continue beating until stiff.
Set whipped cream aside.
Using a glass trifle bowl or other glass bowl,
place a layer of pound cake on bottom of bowl.
Pour some Sherry over pound cake.
Spread some pudding mixture over pound cake.
Place berries over pudding mixture.
Add another layer of pound cake over that.
Sprinkle pound cake with a little more Sherry.
Add more pudding mixture and berries.
Repeat layers until cake, pudding, and berries are used up.

Top with fresh whipped cream.
Add fresh berries and a mint sprig for garnish.
Refrigerate for at least 2 hours before serving.

LEMON CHEESE BARS

My sister and I concocted this recipe years ago, trying to duplicate
the favorite Sara Lee's French Cream Cheese Cake.
We feel it's a good substitution when you can't have the real thing!

CRUST
⅔ cup butter, melted

⅔ cup brown sugar, packed

2 cups all-purpose flour

1 cup finely chopped walnuts or pecans, optional

Melt butter and mix brown sugar, flour and nuts with fork.
Grease and flour a standard size jelly roll pan and
pack 3/4 of mixture in bottom of pan.
Bake at 350 degrees for 15 minutes.

FILLING
16 oz. cream cheese, softened

½ cup granulated sugar

2 eggs

4 Tablespoons milk

2 Tablespoons lemon juice

1 teaspoon vanilla

Beat cream cheese with sugar and add eggs.
Add milk, lemon juice and vanilla and cream well.
Pour into pan over crust and lightly crumble remaining crust as topping.
Bake at 350 degrees for 25 minutes. Cool completely and cut into little squares.

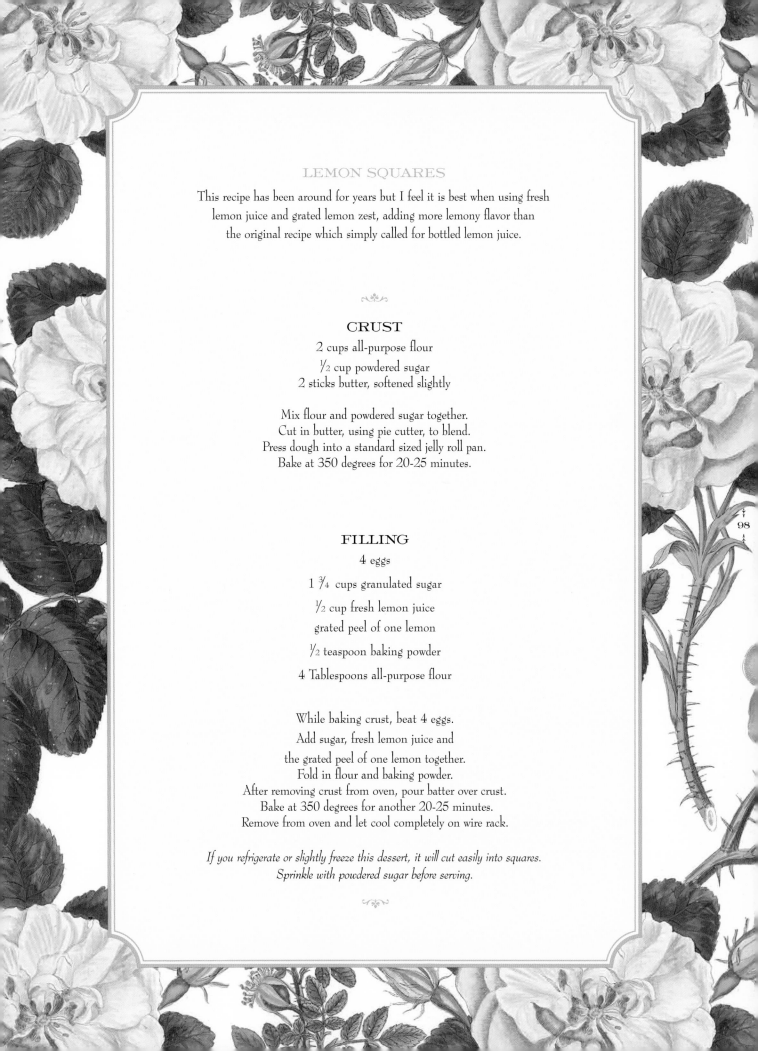

LEMON SQUARES

This recipe has been around for years but I feel it is best when using fresh
lemon juice and grated lemon zest, adding more lemony flavor than
the original recipe which simply called for bottled lemon juice.

❦

CRUST

2 cups all-purpose flour
½ cup powdered sugar
2 sticks butter, softened slightly

Mix flour and powdered sugar together.
Cut in butter, using pie cutter, to blend.
Press dough into a standard sized jelly roll pan.
Bake at 350 degrees for 20-25 minutes.

FILLING

4 eggs

1 ¾ cups granulated sugar

½ cup fresh lemon juice

grated peel of one lemon

½ teaspoon baking powder

4 Tablespoons all-purpose flour

While baking crust, beat 4 eggs.
Add sugar, fresh lemon juice and
the grated peel of one lemon together.
Fold in flour and baking powder.
After removing crust from oven, pour batter over crust.
Bake at 350 degrees for another 20-25 minutes.
Remove from oven and let cool completely on wire rack.

If you refrigerate or slightly freeze this dessert, it will cut easily into squares.
Sprinkle with powdered sugar before serving.

❦

CARROT CAKE

Everyone has their own favorite recipe for carrot cake. This one is mine.
Carrot Cake is good no matter which baking pan you choose to use, so long as
your cake is covered in cream cheese frosting! Baking it in a standard jelly roll pan
allows me to cut the cake into bite-size squares for serving at teatime.
Everyone seems to love Carrot Cake!

❧

1 ¼ cups vegetable oil
2-cups sugar
2-cups grated carrots
4 eggs
3-cups flour
3-teaspoons baking powder
2-teaspoons baking soda
2-teaspoons cinnamon
½ teaspoon salt
¼ cup chopped nuts, optional
1 small can crushed pineapple with juice

❧

Mix oil, sugar and eggs together and beat well using an electric mixer.
Sift flour and all other dry ingredients together in a bowl.
Add carrots to batter with the flour mixture and blend well.
Add pineapple in its own juice and blend well.
Grease and flour a standard size jelly roll baking pan or use small loaf pans.
Pour batter into pan and bake at 350 degrees for 40-45 minutes or until
toothpick inserted into center comes out clean.
Cool completely on wire rack.
*If using a loaf pan, remove cake from pan to cool.
Frost the entire cake with cream cheese frosting.
If using a jelly roll pan, frost cake in the pan.
Then slice and move to a serving platter.

CREAM CHEESE FROSTING

❧⁂☙

¾ cup butter, softened
8 oz. pkg. cream cheese, softened
4 cups powdered sugar
2 teaspoons vanilla

❧⁂☙

Beat together:
butter, cream cheese and powdered sugar
until blended.
Stir in vanilla extract.
If frosting is too stiff to spread, stir in milk,
one teaspoon at a time until desired consistency.

HELPFUL HINTS

Recipes calling for the use of a 9 X 13 inch baking pan, and instead use a standard
jelly roll pan, which is longer, wider, and shorter in depth. Baking time may be
reduced by several minutes when using a jelly roll pan versus deeper baking dishes.
The same holds true when using 6-cup angel food and Bundt cake pans as opposed
to a 12-cup size. Presenting cakes and cookies in miniature versions are
so much more appealing for teatime treats.

CHOCOLATE POUND CAKE

I have been making this recipe for over 25 years and trust me,
it is THE best chocolate pound cake you will ever taste!

~✿~

3 cups all-purpose flour

1 Tablespoon baking powder

¼ teaspoon salt

1 cup butter, softened

3 cups granulated sugar

1 ½ Tablespoons vanilla extract

3 eggs

1 cup unsweetened cocoa powder

*1 ¾ cups milk

~✿~

Preheat oven to 350 degrees.
Sift flour, baking powder and salt together and set aside.
Beat butter and sugar together until fluffy.
Add vanilla.
Add eggs, one at a time, beating well after each addition.
Add cocoa and mix well.
Add milk alternately with dry ingredients until blended.
Grease and flour a 12 cup Bundt pan or two 6 cup Bundt pans.
Bake for 1 hour and 15 minutes or until toothpick inserted comes out clean.
Cool on wire rack at least 15 minutes before removing from pan.
Sprinkle with powdered sugar before serving.
*A can of evaporated milk may be used which equals about 1 ½ cups.
Just add milk to that to equal 1 ¾ cups total.

STRAWBERRY ANGEL FOOD CREAM CAKE

My sister made this cake for a dinner party she held in her home 30 years ago.
I have been making it and serving it to family and friends ever since.

❧

One large Angel Food Cake

Or

Two small Angel Food Cakes or Loaves

1-pint FRESH strawberries

12 oz. COOL WHIP

or fresh whipping cream, fully whipped and sweetened

❧

Bake angel food cake according to directions or buy an angel food cake
from the bakery. Let it cool completely before cutting and tunneling.
Slice strawberries, reserving 5 or 6 berries for garnishing.
Mix 2-cups of COOL WHIP topping or fresh whipped cream
with a couple drops of red food coloring to make the cream pink.
Add sliced strawberries to pink cream.
Cut off top of cake about 2 inches from top and set aside.
Tunnel inside of cake all the way around,
leaving 1 inch on sides and middle.
Take the cream and strawberry mixture and gently spoon
the entire mixture into the cavity of the cake.
Replace the top of the cake.
Frost the entire cake with remaining cream.
Garnish with remaining strawberries.
Refrigerate at least 2 hours before slicing and serving.
You may substitute fresh whole raspberries for strawberries.
You may also use a chocolate angel food cake with fresh raspberries or sliced bananas.

CRUST

3/4 cup graham cracker crumbs

1/4 cup granulated sugar

1/4 cup butter, melted

Mix crumbs, sugar and melted butter together and press into the bottom of
a 10-inch spring-form pan or smaller spring-form pans if you have them.
Set in freezer when done.

FILLING I

2 – 8 oz. Cream cheese, softened

½ cup granulated sugar

3 eggs, room temperature

1 teaspoon vanilla extract

Preheat oven to 375 degrees.
Beat cream cheese several minutes; add eggs, one at a time;
add sugar and vanilla and beat until smooth and creamy.
Remove crust from freezer and pour batter into crust.
Bake for 20-25 minutes or less, until cheese looks "set."
Remove from oven and let cool on rack while preparing next filling.
Set oven at 475 degrees and wait 10 minutes before returning to oven with next filling.

FILLING II

1 pint (2 cups) real sour cream

¼ cup granulated sugar

1 teaspoon vanilla extract

Blend sour cream, sugar and vanilla.
After cake has been out of the oven for 10 minutes,
pour second filling over the cake and return to oven for 10 minutes.
Remove from oven and let cool completely before refrigerating.
Refrigerate overnight or for several hours before serving.
Serve plain or garnish with fresh berries, mint sprigs and whipping cream.

Note: Use a cookie sheet underneath baking pan to catch any butter drippings from crust.

SOUR CREAM POUND CAKE

I don't know anyone who doesn't love pound cake.
This particular recipe is very light and flavorful.
Pound cakes are usually better tasting the day after they are baked.
This is definitely one recipe that may be baked in advance of any party.

❦

1 cup butter, softened
3 cups granulated sugar
6 large eggs
3 cups cake flour
¼ teaspoon baking soda
8 oz. sour cream
1 teaspoon vanilla extract

❦

Beat softened butter at medium speed
for several minutes until smooth and creamy.
Gradually add sugar, beating well for 5 minutes.
Add eggs, one at a time, beating well after each addition.
Combine cake flour and baking soda.
Add to butter mixture, one cup at a time.
With mixer on low speed, add sour cream and vanilla.
Grease and flour a 12-cup Bundt pan or 2 – 6-cup Bundt pans.
Pour batter into pan.
Bake at 300 degrees for 60-90 minutes
or until a pick inserted comes out clean.
Cool for at least ½ hour before removing from pan.
Cook completely on a wire rack.
Sprinkle with powdered sugar and serve plain or with whipped cream and berries!

FRESH FLOWER CAKE

This is a recipe for a "fresh" arrangement that is made to look like a cake.
It was demonstrated at a floral design class I took some years back.
I thought it was a great way to celebrate a special occasion and use the
fresh arrangement as your centerpiece. You may use any color flowers
or any type of flower you wish. However, I will give you the directions
according to how I saw it made.

Materials Needed:
Cylinder-shaped floral foam
Water
Fresh flowers
Flower clipper

Directions:
Take a 6 – 8 inch high floral cylinder by approximately 6 inches in diameter
and soak the floral cylinder in water until it's all absorbed and heavy with the water.
Place the soaked cylinder on a pretty platter or pedestal cake dish.
Start cutting carnations or other flowers of a dark color with about 2 - 3 inch stems
and stick into base of cylinder all the way around until it is "packed" with flowers.
Then add two rows of white carnations or other flowers *(to resemble frosting)*.
As before, cut stems to approximately 2 – 3 inches in length
and continue all the way around the cylinder
until the white flowers are again "packed" into two rows.
This should fill the cylinder all the way to the top.
Decorate the top of the "cake" with roses or any other flowers you wish.
If you spritz arrangement with water everyday it should last 1-2 weeks.

HOMEMADE LEMONADE RECIPE ON PAGE 113

TEA AND BEVERAGE RECIPES

"If you are cold, tea will *warm* you. If you are too heated, it will cool you.
If you are depressed, it will cheer you. If you are excited, it will *calm* you."

-WILLIAM GLADSTONE - BRITISH PRIME MINISTER (1865)

LIKE tea itself, there are countless recipes for creating special beverages to serve with afternoon tea. Once you have mastered making great tea and lemonade, the mixing of other ingredients in combination with these drinks only help to enhance the various blends. Fruited tea punches were popular and recorded as early as the 17th century, and were often spiked with rum, brandy, or other liquors.

A GLASS of sherry or champagne is an added luxury and simply irresistible when served with afternoon tea! Although Americans drink more coffee than anywhere else in the world, I personally choose not to serve coffee at teatime. I sincerely hope you will try some of these other suggested beverages and create recipes that I feel are more symbolic and refreshing for celebrating teatime. The greatest thing about serving tea, lemonade, non-alcoholic fruit punches, and sparkling beverages is that they seem to satisfy all ages and are the perfect accompaniments to daytime or evening refreshments.

For bottled sparkling beverages I have two favorite suppliers that I highly recommend: IMPORTED KRISTIAN REGALE is bottled in a variety of outstanding fruit flavors such as pear, apple, peach, and black current. MARTINELLI'S also offers a wide variety of fruited beverages with their Sparkling Cider as their signature Gold Medal favorite.

I TRY to keep a couple of bottles of sparkling beverages on hand at all times. Children love it more than soda pop, especially when it is presented to them in stemmed glassware; after all, presentation is everything and a little formality makes guests feel so special!

TEA & BEVERAGE RECIPES

❧❧❦

Liquid Sugar

Homemade Lemonade

Black Iced Tea with Fresh Fruits & Berries

Quick and Easy Fruit Sparkler

Tea and Lemonade Punch

Lemonade and Pineapple Punch

Citrus Wine Cooler

Fruited Champagne Punch

❧❧❦

IN my previous chapter, titled, PREPARING TEA, I give instructions to prepare a gallon of iced tea. Some of my favorite tea blends for making great iced tea are:

ORANGE PEKOE · DARJEELING · EARL GREY · BLACK CURRENT

I FEEL Earl Grey and Black Current can stand on their own and only require ice cubes and perhaps a lemon slice or a little sugar if you prefer your iced tea sweetened, otherwise, unflavored black blends could be combined with some of the recipes described on page 114.

LIQUID SUGAR

Liquid Sugar is so easy to make. The first time I was introduced to it was
while enjoying lunch at The Williamsburg Inn in Williamsburg, Virginia.
The liquid sugar was served in individual mini pitchers along with each glass of iced tea.
Because I am so fond of anything in miniature form, I immediately went
shopping for similar pitchers and have been serving iced tea in this same fashion
ever since! No more granules will be left on the bottom of your iced tea glass!

1 cup granulated sugar
1 cup boiled water

After water has come to a boil, stir in sugar until dissolved.
Remove from heat and let cool completely.
Refrigerate for up to 3 weeks.
Use a small amount per serving or according to taste.

For larger crowds, liquid sugar is especially elegant when it is served in
a small pitcher on a serving tray, using a paper doily as a liner.
Add some mint leaves and colorful fruit slices to garnish the tray, or
use individual mini pitchers at each place setting as suggested above.
Either way, your guests will be impressed!

HOMEMADE LEMONADE

When visiting my grandmother in Florida,
she made me what she called "old fashion lemonade."
This is how she prepared it:

Cut 12 lemons in half and remove seeds.
Squeeze the juice of the lemons into a gallon-size pitcher.
Add ½ cup sugar, stirring until sugar dissolves.
Place the lemons in the pitcher with the liquid mixture.
Fill the pitcher with ice.
Let stand at room temperature until all the ice melts.
Remove all the lemon halves and pour the lemonade over ice in glasses.
Garnish with fresh lemon slices and sprigs of fresh mint.

BLACK ICED TEA *with* FRESH FRUITS *&* BERRIES

Start with a good black tea blend.

❧

After you have made your iced tea, add fresh lemon slices, orange slices,
fresh berries, mint sprigs, or any combo thereof
directly into the pitcher of iced tea.

❧

Not only does this make an appealing presentation, the juice and rinds
of the lemons and oranges add a lot of flavor to the tea.
Strawberries, black raspberries, and red raspberries also produce
added flavor and color while looking attractive floating in the tea.
You may prefer to add slices of fruits and berries to
individual glasses instead of placing them in the pitcher itself.

QUICK AND EASY FRUIT SPARKLER

1 liter (33.8 oz) bottle of sparkling mineral or seltzer water
1 can of your favorite frozen fruit juice concentrate, mostly thawed

Place the fruit juice concentrate in the bottom of a large pitcher.
Slowly add the liter of sparkling or seltzer water and stir gently.
Add lots of ice and garnish with mint leaves or
place fresh berries in individual glasses.

TEA AND LEMONADE PUNCH

8 quality black tea bags
3 quarts boiling water
½ cup granulated sugar
32 oz bottle ginger ale, chilled
12 oz of lemonade

Once water has reached a boil, remove from heat source
and place tea bags in water to steep for 10 minutes.
Remove tea bags and add sugar, stirring until dissolved.
Add lemonade and chill. Pour into a large punch bowl.
Just before serving, add chilled ginger ale.

Garnish punch bowl with floating lemon slices.
Garnish individual punch cups or glasses
with a lemon slice and mint sprig.

116

HELPFUL HINTS

Add a touch of elegance by using stemware when serving sparkling beverages.

LEMONADE AND PINEAPPLE PUNCH

~·❖·~

1 ½ gallons lemonade, chilled
2 – 48 oz cans pineapple juice, chilled
3 liters lemon-lime soda, chilled

~·❖·~

Refrigerate lemonade.
Chill pineapple juice and lemon-lime soda.
Pour lemonade and pineapple juice into a large punch bowl.
Gently stir in lemon-lime soda.

*Note: You may make ice cubes out of lemonade
to use in the punch so as not to dilute the punch.*

CITRUS WINE COOLER

2 cups orange juice, chilled
6 oz can frozen lemonade concentrate, thawed
1 cup orange-flavored liqueur
1 bottle of your favorite white wine, chilled
1 liter club soda, chilled

Combine first four ingredients in a large punch bowl, stirring gently.
Add club soda and some crushed ice, stirring gently.
Garnish punch bowl with floating orange slices.

FRUITED CHAMPAGNE PUNCH

10 oz. package frozen red raspberries, partially thawed
8 oz. can crushed pineapple, chilled
12 oz. can frozen lemonade concentrate, thawed
2 quarts champagne, chilled

Blend raspberries and pineapple in a blender or food processor, until smooth.
Add lemonade concentrate just to blend.
Pour into a large punch bowl. Gently stir in champagne.
*Note: Lemon-lime soda may replace champagne
if you prefer a non-alcoholic beverage.*

ACKNOWLEDGEMENTS

I HAVE ALWAYS KNOWN that it takes more than a little luck and determination to put ideas into motion. For me it took an array of people who encouraged and supported my efforts. With that said, I would like to thank those who have influenced my life in some way or another or to those responsible for helping me realize a dream come true with the publishing of this book.

Let me begin by thanking my husband and life-long partner, Ray, for supporting me, encouraging me, praising my efforts and for making it possible for me to follow my dreams.

A grateful heart goes to my daughter, Katie, whose love and support keeps me focused on what is most important and who so willingly and patiently spent her entire childhood helping me run my tea business.

❋

Thom Rouse, whose photographs for this book captured the essence of afternoon teas.

Special thanks to Anna Griffin of Anna Griffin, Inc. for her enthusiasm, advice, design work, and outstanding artwork for this project.

Holley Silirie, Anna's art director, and Stephanie Haller, designer for assisting in this project.

❋

Martha Whitaker and Patricia Turley at Dorrance Publishing for their guidance in helping to bring my book to publication.

Meghan Reinke for helping edit the first draft of my manuscript.

❋

Mr. John Harney of Harney & Sons Fine Teas, for his wit and wisdom in setting the records straight for pertinent tea information used in this book.

My sisters-in-law, Pamela Spalding, Julie Enno and Lyn Acocella-Bagley for their love and support.

My friend and editor at TEA a Magazine, Pearl Dexter, who invited me to attend her tea school and encouraged me to continue writing and talking about tea.

Vicki Matranga, for her interest and for supplying me with historical information.

❋

Don and Katherine from Robbins Florist in St. Charles, Illinois for providing me with beautiful floral arrangements for our photographs.

❋

Pat and Steve Burnham of The Paper Merchant in Geneva, Illinois, who have for 20 years been helpful in selecting just the right words for printed invitations.

❋

My niece and attorney, Meredith Wilson, who willingly guided me through this project and shares my love of entertaining.

Phyllis Rindone, my big sister, mentor, and best friend, who initially introduced me to entertaining with style and living graciously while encouraging and supporting my every effort.

My brothers, Tom, Bob, and Chuck Bagley for their unconditional love, support, and encouragement in everything I have ever done.

My mother, Corinne, who first influenced my organizational skills, domestic skills, and culinary interests.

In loving memory of my father, James A. Bagley, for instilling family values while insisting on impeccable manners at all times.

In loving memory of Thelma and Ray Shafer, both of whom always supported me and shared many a cuppa with Katie and me.

❋

Dawn and Lynn Wilson, both of whom have supported my efforts and share my love of English teatime.

❋

Many thanks to our precious friends and traveling buddies, Sharon, Mallory, and Rob McCool, whose love and support add new meaning to the phrase "extended family."

❋

Two of my dearest friends and original tea-drinking companions, Cheryl and Rita Fabek, who have encouraged and cheered me on from the very beginning.

❋

My favorite cb's, Shirley Nichol, Nancy Reinke, and "Peppermint" Patti Kendrick, whose loving friendship and whacky humor have given new meaning to many memorable tea time occasions.

❋

My girlfriends Kathy Stickney & Jeanne Fennessy who have encouraged and supported me from the beginning when talking tea shop and writing a book about tea was only an idea.

Miss Arlene Hawbaker, my friend, talented crafter, gourmet cook, and baker, who helped me in both of my tea shops.

❊

My friends Linda Steele and Amy Steele-Harris, who have experienced many tea time adventures and educational trips with me while finding humor in sipping iced tea and eating deviled eggs with Katie and me in the pouring rain.

❊

Miss Vicki and Valerie Stokes, my girlfriends and traveling companions who have literally jumped off of cliffs to have tea with me.

❊

My very dear and generous friends, Konnie and Dr. Earl Medeiros, for their encouragement and support.

❊

Diana Dean, Cherri Fiorenza and their mother Lillian Gardener-Croft, my friends and favorite tea ladies at Taste, a tea salon in Williamsburg, Virginia.

❊

Rosa Lea Meadows and Sharon Berg, whose friendships have always made taking tea together so delightful.

❊

Denise Bischof-Hamester, my very first and forever friend

Gay Lynn Maise and Megan Maise who enjoy tea and friendship any time.

❊

Sue Jaeger-Mitchell, Stephanie Mitchell, Carol Cummins, and Caroline Carter for sharing friendship, tea, and art in many forms.

❊

Cathy Leone, Helen Wilbur, Andy Galloway, and Evonne Wilkinson for their friendship and many memorable tea time adventures.

❊

Hannah & Sarah Kurath, my little tea ladies who now call Colorado their home.

❊

My friend, Judith Siwek, who shares my love of all things tea-related.

❊

My friend and professional floral designer, Tammy Pocklington, whose lovely arrangements graced both of my teashops.

❊

Janice Rojek-Pecka, my childhood and life-long friend

Denise Campbell, my special friend and attentive listener.

❊

Rosalie Giurato for her loving friendship…. Merci!

❊

Lynn Brandys, one of the best designers ever, who gave me the opportunity to further develop my design skills and who shared the onset of my tea adventures by taking tea with me at The Plaza Hotel in New York.

❊

In loving memory of Judy Preissner, who valued friendship and a good chat which always extended long beyond afternoon teatime. Happy trails to you until we meet again.

❊

Betsy Lichner, my former neighbor, friend and exceptional hostess, who feels comfortable sharing tea with me while wearing pajamas!

❊

And last but not least, remembering our devoted four-legged companion, little Annie, who faithfully watched over both of my tea shops, greeted customers and sat beside me throughout the writing of this book.

❊

I thank you ALL, from the bottom of my heart!